Praise for *Simplicity*

Rohr has a unique ability to present a radical, up-to-date, prophetic call to his listeners while assuring them of God's all-embracing love. *—The Mennonite*

Once again Rohr presents his prophetic message with authority, sincerity, and strength. *—Sisters Today*

We encounter Rohr at his best, offering insightful comments on a wide variety of issues, from feminism to the men's movement, from the Enneagram to the Twelve Steps. *—Spiritual Book News*

You'll find much here to enrich the daily attempt to live a Christian life. *—Praying*

It will assist those who are struggling to find meaning in personal prayer, but do not know where to turn when their own words fail or cannot speak the deepest desires of their souls. *—PBF*

Also by Richard Rohr

Everything Belongs, 1999, revised and updated edition, 2003

Called, Formed, Sent, with Thomas C. Welch, 2002

The Enneagram: A Christian Perspective, with Andreas Ebert, 2001

Hope Against Darkness: The Transforming Vision of St. Francis of Assisi in an Age of Anxiety, with John Bookser Feister, 2001

The Good News According to Luke: Spiritual Reflections, 1997

Jesus' Plan for a New World: The Sermon on the Mount, with John Bookser Feister, 1996

Job and the Mystery of Suffering: Spiritual Reflections, 1996

Enneagram II: Advancing Spiritual Discernment, 1995

Radical Grace: Daily Meditations, 1995

Quest for the Grail, 1994

Near Occasions of Grace, 1993

Experiencing the Enneagram, with Andreas Ebert et al., 1992

The Wild Man's Journey: Reflections on Male Spirituality, revised edition (with Joseph Martos), 1992, 1996

Simplicity: The Art of Living, 1991

Discovering the Enneagram: An Ancient Tool for a New Spiritual Journey, with Andreas Ebert, 1990

Why Be Catholic?: Understanding our Experience and Tradition, with Joseph Martos, 1989

The Great Themes of Scripture: New Testament, with Joseph Martos, 1988

The Great Themes of Scripture: Old Testament, with Joseph Martos, 1987

SIMPLICITY

The Freedom of
Letting Go

Revised and
Updated Edition

Richard Rohr

Translated by
Peter Heinneg

A Crossroad Book
The Crossroad Publishing Company
New York

The Crossroad Publishing Company
www.CrossroadPublishing.com

Originally published under the title *Von der Freiheit loszulassen –
Letting Go,* translated and introduced by Andreas Ebert © Claudius
Verlag Munich 1990

English translation copyright © 1991
by The Crossroad Publishing Company

Revised English-language edition copyright © 2003
by The Crossroad Publishing Company

This book is typeset in 11/15 Optima.

Printed in the United States of America

Library of Congress Cataloging-in-Publication Data
Rohr, Richard.
    [Von der Freiheit loszulassen. English]
    Simplicity : the freedom of letting go / Richard Rohr ; translated by
Peter Heinegg.
       p. cm.
    ISBN 0-8245-2115-3 (alk. paper)
    1. Simplicity – Religious aspects – Christianity.   I. Title.
BV4647.S48R6413 2003
252'.02 – dc22
                                2003017600

10   11 10

For the little ones everywhere,
who hold before the world the secrets
of the ever-coming Christ.

For the family, friars, and friends
who gave me the eyes and heart
to recognize their simple secret.

These are only hints and guesses,
Hints followed by guesses;
And the rest is prayer, observance, discipline,
Thought and action.
The hint half guessed, the gift half understood,
Is Incarnation.

—"The Dry Salvages," T. S. Eliot

O Lord, don't ever let us move into stone houses.

—A poor man in Nairobi

Contents

Foreword

A FTER A LONG ABSENCE Richard Rohr returned to the German-speaking world. His subjects have remained the same as ever — and yet there are new tones here. Richard Rohr is discovering more and more the contemplative side of faith, the process of becoming empty and letting go, as Meister Eckhart and the German mystics in particular preached and practiced it. Once again we are taken along on an exciting journey, once again we are challenged not only to rethink things, but to live in a new and different way.[1]

Two Voices from Switzerland

One: It was said of Jesus that he spoke with authority and not like the doctors of the law. For he taught from his soul, from his life and his experience. Also from what he had learned and understood in his meetings with children, women, and men, with the "devil," but also with his Father in heaven. When you meet somebody who also teaches "with authority," who has something to say, who senses what his audience's current concerns are because they concern himself, then you get the feeling that you already knew what you just heard. "Actually there was nothing new. I've felt that before too; it's just that I couldn't put it into words before." We don't feel stupid — but like people who already know what we have heard. We have

11

been encouraged to rely on ourselves, to listen to ourselves, and to trust what we hear, sense, and guess there.
For we all have within us the real teacher and master. Jesus
calls her the Holy Spirit, who will lead us to all truth. This
doesn't mean that we don't need one another anymore,
but that we can stop looking for the master and hanging
on the lips of a teacher. That may still be necessary when
we're children, but mature persons heed the teacher in
their hearts.

Nevertheless teachers have been given to us who can
strengthen us with their words and enable us to hear
with our outer ears what life and the Holy Spirit have
long wanted to teach us. Richard Rohr's words have given
courage and hope to many people. After hearing Fr. Rohr
someone said: "This time I didn't leave with the feeling,
'Now you've got to do this and that too, and then it'll
be good.' I wasn't driven to more achievement, but to
more trust: Let go, trust in God, trust in life, and what it
teaches you."

Rohr doesn't teach passivity but active trust, action and
contemplation, commitment in the world, and the ability to let go in God. One beautiful experience for me
was that much of what has become important for me
in the last few years — what for some is still tarred with
the brush of liberation theology, feminism, New Age, or
worse — was treated by Rohr the Franciscan as old, simple,
joyful Franciscan theology, if we may label it theology at
all. Perhaps it's better to call it the simple joy in God, in
Jesus Christ, in creation and creatures that became per-
ceptible in the spirit of Brother Francis. This wasn't the

Zeitgeist speaking, but the spirit of Jesus and the Sermon on the Mount.[2]

❧

Two: Filled with Gospel "enthusiasm" Fr. Rohr challenged his listeners to risk taking a look at the Church that could be but isn't (yet). It was impressive to hear this man, without excuses and digressions, point out and admit that Western Christian bourgeois consumer culture is much closer than the Reign of God. So in this sense our present-day Christianity is frighteningly infected by the viruses of "wealth," "security," and "national egoism." But on the other hand it is possible to remain bound in love to this Church and its tradition. This sort of attitude is often scarcely understood. Anyone who relentlessly unmasks the real existing situation is easily labeled a complainer, a befouler of his own nest. But it's precisely the ones who poke a critical nose into things who have kept alive a special love for their Church or the country they live in. They intrude precisely because it's important that their Church or country doesn't go off on any old path. I hope we learn to give more of a welcome to these voices of unpleasant meddling, especially in the Church. They might be prophetic voices.

Richard Rohr paraphrases a saying of Augustine, that "many belong to the Church who don't belong to God, but many belong to God who don't belong to the Church." As if this saying had needed an illustration, the following episode occurred: A man, who didn't exactly correspond to our notion of the average churchgoer, quite obviously not pampered by life, with an old-fashioned artificial leg and wearing an unconventional suit, walked cautiously with his large dog down the center aisle of the church. Passing the astonished public he silently placed a burning candle in front of the pulpit, and then quietly sat down along the side aisle. I wish there were more such openness, such natural ease in the church.[3]

ANDREAS EBERT

Preface

❦

THE MYTHS OF MODERNISM are dying all around us. Our sophistication and complexity are self-destructing. For several hundred years we were convinced in the West that progress, human reason, and higher technology would resolve the human dilemma. They clearly have not. Without denying the gifts of mind and science, we now doubt their messianic promise. More analysis does not necessarily mean more wisdom, and having more options is not necessarily freedom. The accumulation of things is not likely to bring more happiness, and time saved is rarely used for contemplation.

Progress has too often been achieved at the expense of the earth, and human reason has too easily legitimated war, greed, and the pursuit of a private agenda, while technology pays those who serve it, especially the moguls of militarism and medicine. Our philosophy of progress has led us to trust in our own limitlessness and in our future more than in the quality and the mystery of the *now*. Religion at its best is always concerned with the depth and breadth and wonder of things. In this sense we have become an impatient and irreligious people. The paschal mystery, the yin and yang of all reality, is outshouted by the quite recent and unproven slogan: "we can have it all!"

T. S. Eliot struggles with this chosen blindness in his fourth quartet, "Little Gidding":

15

Not known, because not looked for
But heard, half-heard, in the stillness
Between two waves of the sea.
Quick now, here, now, always —
A condition of complete simplicity
(Costing not less than everything)

✴ The cost, of course, is the problem. The almost impossible task of the Church is to offer both the promise
and the price — simultaneously. Promise without price
becomes sweet sentimentality; price without promise becomes shame, burden, and grief. We have enough of both.
But who will point us back to the "condition of complete
simplicity"? And who wants to go there? I do believe there
is a divine therapy both for the individual and for the
Church. It is the radical contemplative stance. Aldous Hux-
ley rightly called it "the perennial philosophy." It is the
return to simplicity that comes from much good looking
and good listening. I will go so far as to say, *There is no
other way.* But the cost is not less than everything:

To come to the pleasure you have not
you must go by a way in which you enjoy not.
To come to the knowledge you have not
you must go by a way in which you know not.
To come to the possession you have not
you must go by a way in which you possess not.
To come to be what you are not
you must go by a way in which you are not.

St. John of the Cross[4]

That is lost wisdom, yet it recurs in every age and in every religion. But reason would never lead us there, and certainly not a philosophy of progress, efficiency, or "self-actualization." It comes by "revelation." It is waited for, needed, desired, and received as wondrous grace. It is never logically concluded. That's why Jesus says that it is only *faith* that "saves."

My understanding has been slow in coming. I now see that it is just as hard for the Church to believe as it is for the individual. I am really not sure which comes first, but right now they are both pointing accusing fingers at one another to avoid their own treacherous journey. I know that the Church body cannot ask of its members what it has not exemplified; and the members cannot ask of the Body what they will not risk themselves. Who goes first? The divine alchemy of history never tells us for sure. Did More and Newman form the English church or did the English church form them? I don't suppose that we need to know. "Not to us, O God, not to us, but to your name give the glory." (Ps. 115:1)

And same for the blame. The amorphous guilt must go somewhere. We used to accuse ourselves mercilessly, and now we do the same to parents, institutions, or history itself. There must be a victim and a victimizer. But why? What does it help? Maybe that is why Jesus became the cosmic victim and refused to condemn the victimizers: "They know not what they do." (Luke 23:34)

We are ready and so in need of mercy. The painful mystery of things, the injustice of it all, the mixed blessing, just *is*. Nothing is gained by accusing or avoiding, except a false sense of control. History is ours and we are history —

all of it. The Church might best be described as the place where that can honestly happen, where *all* of history can be carried, and carried toward redemption. To isolate any part, or to isolate the whole in favor of a part, is to maim and deface the Body of Christ. It is also to refuse our part in the great human experiment.

To believe in the ongoing mystery of the Church is to be willing to work with history, its level of consciousness, its issues, at this chronological moment on this planet. I will not refuse my place in the great chain of Being; I will live now "for better for worse, for richer for poorer, till death do us part." That is our concrete marriage to Christ. And what other Christ can we meet? What other Christ (or Church) did we expect? What pagan hubris allows us to think that we can jump ahead or stubbornly hide in the past?

But I must also admit that I have never found it harder to believe in the Church. God's redemption of history seems so utterly slow, ineffective, and even impeded by the Church politic. Is three steps forward and two backward the only way to proceed? Somebody is very patient, certainly more than I. Bishops sanctimoniously proclaim their pro-life stance and calmly sanction the murder of Iraqis by the U.S. government. They claim to be certain about God's will in regard to birth control, married priests, women priests, and all manner of sexual conduct (about which Jesus says little or nothing) and yet live in comfortable doubt about God's will in regard to war, riches, and nonviolence (about which Jesus is absolutely clear). This is magisterium? The pope appoints echo-chamber bishops throughout the world, controls the minutiae of a universal, multicultural church, and yet still hopes to speak with authority about Providence, social justice, and trust in God. It just doesn't sell anymore.

But we as individuals are no better. Liberals consider obedience and surrender an affront to their freedom and "wholeness." Conservatives make freedom a bad word, while living on full bended knee before the free market and the supposed freedom of America. Patriarchs live in naive ignorance of their privileged state, while ideological feminists read all of human history through one self-serving paradigm. Lay boards and communities show all of the triumphalism and ego-tripping that the clergy once mastered. How is anyone supposed to see the glorious face of Christ in the midst of such smallness and disbelief? Why would anyone accept evangelization from a people so divided and with such little good news?

But "to whom else shall we go?" (John 6:68) This question is as difficult to answer today as it was in Jesus' time. Individualism leads to eccentricity and arrogance, modern spiritual eclectics finally become articulate narcissists, and cultural gadflies move with every trendy breeze. I have worked with too many Native Americans to buy the pseudo-Indian spirituality that floats around New Mexico, and I appreciate the creation spirituality of my Franciscan tradition too much to think that it was just discovered in California. Even the much needed Twelve Step programs have become their own kind of addiction and avoidance of the painful mystery of things. Let's face it, there is no support group, therapy, theology, or mystic ceremony that is going to take all the pain away.

Even if I had a great gift for writing, your reading experience wouldn't take the mystery away either. But I believe in the truth of the basic Gospel more than ever, and so I am compelled to preach and teach, which I hope will resolve a few contemporary obstacles so that the Gospel can again be gospel, good news *for all the peoples.* (Mark 11:17) I hope it will help you distinguish between the two naivetés: the first is dangerous simplicity — uncritical and unconnected; the second naiveté is blessed simplicity — calm, knowing, patient, self-forgetful because all has been remembered. It is the latter state of simplicity that reinvents the Gospel in every age.

Some years ago I was writing while recovering from unexpected surgery for malignant melanoma. I thought my life on this earth was over, and I was asking God why. I could not deny that I have had a most wonderful life: rich, varied, "full measure, pressed down, shaken together, running over, and poured into my lap." (Luke 6:38) Just when I thought I had said yes, Someone said no, and for now I live again. Is there more room in my lap? Is there room in God's? I'll bet there is. There is always enough room for simplicity.

FR. RICHARD ROHR, O.F.M.
Center for Action and Contemplation
Albuquerque, New Mexico

1

God the Father —
God the Mother?

❧

WHENEVER WE DISCUSS THE IMAGE OF GOD, there's always a lot of controversy and misunderstanding.[5] It takes a long time for us to allow God to be who God really is. Our natural egocentricity wants to make God — and all other people, for that matter — into who we want them or need them to be. It's the role of the prophet to keep people free for God. But at the same time it's the responsibility of the prophet to keep God free for people.

I'd like to begin with something that looks like a cliché: the First Commandment. It says that we're not supposed to make any images of God or to worship them. We've never taken the First Commandment seriously. God created human beings after God's own image, and we've returned the compliment, so to speak, creating God after our image. Thus God or the gods were, as a rule, turned into a mirror image and projection of our own selves. In the end we produced what was typically a kind of tribal god. In America God looks like Uncle Sam, or Santa Claus, or in any case a white Anglo-Saxon. In England, God evokes the British Empire. A Swiss God, perhaps, resembles a banker or a psychologist.

Normally we find it very, very difficult to let God be, a God who's greater than our culture and our projections.

In patriarchal Europe we prefer to see God as a man. And yet it says right there in Genesis: "God created humankind in God's own image; male and female God created them." (Gen. 1:27) That says point blank that God cannot be strictly masculine. And still we seem to need more proof.

Despite all our theology, when this sort of question arises the dominant culture normally carries the day. Or rather, what ultimately prevails is the human ego. We always seem to find a way to keep things firmly in our grasp. And so we've created "God" to go on playing our game: a God who fits into our system. A God who stands outside our system and calls to us is something we can't endure. Thus, for example, we've continually required a God who likes to play war just as much as we do. We've required a domineering God, because we ourselves like to dominate. And since we're so fixated on this, we've almost completely forgotten and ignored what Jesus told us about the nature of God.

At first glance the First Commandment deals only with carved or handmade likenesses of God. But it refers above all to those images of God that we hold in our heads. The great figures of faith are always letting go of their momentary, self-related images of God. But that calls for a high degree of distance from oneself. Perhaps that's why faith is so rare and religion so widespread: because religion is very often a means to maintain our familiar image of God, even when it's pathological and destructive. We feel better with what we know, even when it does us in.

But faith always invites us to a new and unfamiliar place. Thus we can see in the Book of Exodus how the Israelites preferred to go back to slavery in Egypt rather than be led into the wilderness, where they didn't have God in the palm of their hands. As we grow, our image of God and our self-image normally move forward on parallel tracks. And if one of the two breaks down, the other has to come apart too. We stick to both of them, and both stick together. Every crisis of faith implies that one or the other side is cracking up. If you are truly to grow in faith, then in my opinion this process of disintegration ought to take place at least every two or three years. This is the darkness of faith: when you've had to drop the old for a time but haven't yet found the new. It's the terrible space in between, where nobody wants to live. We want to retreat to a spot where I know who I am and who God is — even when our self-image and our image of God destroy each other, which often happens.

The journey of faith demands that we let go of our image of God and our image of ourselves. But we can't do that in our head or on our own; it's done *to* us. The only thing we have to do is live, but live openly and honestly, letting the truth of the world get through to us. We're not converted in our heads or by sermons from the pastor: we're converted by circumstances — if we really let the circumstances speak to us. And when we let reality get through to us, then conversion doesn't take very long. The Santa Claus image of God stops working, and the masculine image of God doesn't last very long either.

Since we need a license to hurl thunderbolts, we've created a Zeus-god who hurls them too. But as soon as we go on an inner journey and discover a place of tenderness and softness, full of compassion, broad and vast, the Zeus-image of God no longer works. Jesus went into the wilderness for forty days, (Matt. 4:2) where he got rid of his images. He was emptied. And that's the real meaning of fasting: to be emptied of your own images. Only when Jesus was emptied of his self-image could the Father give him a new image and call him "dear son." And we can't deny that Jesus was pleased to call his God "father."

Presumably that also had something to do with his patriarchal culture, even if he did dare to call his God "abba" (the word little boys used, like "papa" or "daddy" in Western culture). It probably also says a lot about his human father, Joseph, and about his relationship with him. But Jesus' parables and metaphors often use father-God images we would call feminine. This is especially true of the story of the prodigal son (Luke 15:11–32) as well as when Jesus says that God would gladly be a hen and take us under his wings like little chicks. (Matt. 23:27)

> **As we grow, our image of God and our self-image normally move forward on parallel tracks.**

Retreats and counseling for priests are a main feature of my work. And although these men know a great deal about theology, I've found to my surprise that their image of God is ninety percent a mixture of the image of their own mothers and fathers. And for some reason they themselves are always amazed when they discover this. If their mother was harshly critical, so is their God. If their father was distant and cold, likewise their God is distant and cold.

I would encourage you to examine the extent to which this applies to your life as well.

Again, we have to break through the images to find who God really is. I promise you there's nothing to be afraid of here. But you have no basis to believe that until you take the journey yourself. People who pray always know that. People who empty themselves in the wilderness always meet a God who is greater than they would have dared to hope. The American Trappist monk Thomas Merton, a man who had a great deal of influence on me, describes this experience as "mercy, within mercy, within mercy."[6] There's always a lot of anxiety and insecurity in letting go of your current images of yourselves and your images of God. Only God can lead you, and all you can do is let go. The spiritualities of all great world religions teach us letting go, or how to step aside.

I believe that we have, especially in the northern European countries, transformed the Gospel into self-control. On the other hand I'm convinced that the Gospel itself is about self-surrender. Self-control is a masculine way of thinking. But self-surrender is perhaps rather a feminine form of thinking. We haven't allowed God to teach us to surrender.

One of the dominant peer group movements in America is comprised of Twelve Step programs. The concept was created more than a half century ago by a man named Bill Wilson, when he founded Alcoholics Anonymous. While the Church talks about self-control, these groups talk about self-surrender. They don't gather in rectangular churches with a pulpit in the middle. The pulpit symbolizes the centrality of the sermon, which normally *enthrones* the left hemisphere of the brain, the more masculine kind of think-ing. Twelve Step group members gather in a circle, and the participants share their pain with one another. No therapist comes in to psychoanalyze them, and no minister comes in to pray over them. When people share their trust and their pain, it's purely and simply the mystery of the naked body of Christ.

When people get together in solidarity and unity, not out of power but out of powerlessness, then Christ is in their midst. And honestly, I find a lot more healing in these simple groups than in most of our churches. I also have a sense of these gatherings as having a much more cultur-ally feminine image of God: God as a healer, as one who participates and doesn't just think — which is not to say that women are always healing and men are always think-ing; I know these are stereotypes, but for whatever reason, stereotypes that are rather common cross-culturally.

Like many other people I've continually wondered why Jesus came to us as a man and why he chose twelve men as disciples. I have only my interpretation for this and no proof that it's right. But I think that if Jesus had come as a woman, and had this woman been forgiving and compassionate, and had she taught nonviolence, we wouldn't have expe-rienced that as revelation. "Oh, well, a typical woman," we would have said. But the fact that a man in a patriar-chal society took on these qualities that we call "feminine" was a breakthrough in revelation. So he spent three years teaching twelve men how to do things differently — and they almost never caught on. And for two thousand years many men in the Church have never caught on, because we men wanted a God of domination. We've needed a

God who would allow the Germans to kill the French and the French to kill the English. A feminine God wouldn't have gotten the job done. The Sermon on the Mount was oft neglected. In the men's Church there is little room for turning the other cheek and forgiving one's enemies.

Ever since the Sermon on the Mount, the Gospel and Western civilization have been on a collision course. But the collision course turned into a one-way street. And the winner wasn't Jesus; the winner was Western civilization. We've taken Jesus over and placed a crown on his head, not a crown of thorns, but a royal crown, which he expressly rejected. But we need kings to keep England, France, and all the other countries in line. Especially after the Edict of Milan in 313, when Constantine made Christianity the established religion of the Roman Empire, we have read the Gospels from the perspective of power instead of from the side of the poor and the disestablished.

So he taught his twelve apostles how it could be done differently. We see, for example, in the Gospel of Mark how he tells his disciples three times: we must die, we must lose, we must be powerless. And each time they either don't get it or they change the subject. And the last one to catch on is Peter, the so-called Prince of the Apostles. (By the way, this is also the only time Jesus calls one of his beloved disciples a "devil," (Mark 8:33) implying "You haven't understood at all what I'm after.")

Until the end of Mark's Gospel it's always the men who don't understand what Jesus is talking about. The women, on the other hand, always understand. And the first witness to the resurrection is not a man, but a woman who was considered a sinner, Mary Magdalen. For the Church's first thousand years she was called an apostle. This can now be proven from liturgical texts. She was even called the "apostle to the apostles." The fact that she *was* just that is clear from all four Gospels.

The Gospel text reveals the beginnings of the bias against women. Mary Magdalene and the women are not taken seriously as witnesses by the apostles, even though the text also reveals what they could not deny: after the Resurrection, Jesus reveals himself to Mary Magdalene first, and *she was sent first to those who became the official witnesses.* The Gospel is a portent of what really was to happen: we would have a hard time with a feminine face for God, a God of ordinary human contact, a God who is a lover instead of a God who is merely known intellectually. Where did Jesus learn to wash the feet of his apostles? (John 13:5) In the previous chapter his own feet are washed by a woman, Mary of Bethany! (12:3) This is no theology located in the head, but a theology that feels at ease in the body.

I've had the wonderful experience of preaching in almost all the parts of the world. And it's becoming increasingly clear to me that people in different parts of the world feel comfortable in different parts of the body. The population of Europe undoubtedly feels most at ease in the head, while the Africans, for example, perhaps feel most at ease in their bodies without all the shame that most of us sense when we look at our bodies. I believe that if we had a more feminine image of God, we wouldn't have the terrible problems with authority and sexuality to struggle with in our Church and culture.

During the Middle Ages we attempted to even out the masculine/feminine imbalance through the image of Mary.

We Catholics have often exaggerated her significance. It may have been bad theology to treat Mary as if she were God, but it was very good and even necessary psychology. We needed a feminine face for God. From the eleventh to the thirteenth centuries most of the churches in Europe were called "Notre Dame" or "Frauenkirche." It was as if the whole soul were longing for a God as tender and gentle as Mary was.

The journey of faith demands that we let go of our image of God and our image of ourselves. But we can't do that in our head or on our own; it's done *to* us. The only thing we have to do is live, but live openly and honestly, letting the truth of the world get through to us.

I remember a time when I was a little boy in Kansas. Our priests and nuns, who came from Ireland, tried to encourage us little Catholics to pray the rosary. They said: "When you get to heaven, St. Peter will be standing there at the gate. Of course, he's got the key, but he's a man. And you can peek through the gate, and there you see Jesus, but he's a man too. And then you look past Jesus, and there sits the old man on the throne." But, these good Irish sisters said, "There's a secret entrance way" — nowadays this will sound super-Catholic and extremely heretical — "Go to the back entrance to heaven! If you're a good boy, and you've prayed your rosary, Mary will be at the back window, and the rosary will hang down and pull you up into heaven."

Horrible theology — but a good idea, once you understand it, because most people grew up with conditional love from their father and unconditional love from their mother. Actually that wasn't true for me: I have a good German-born mother, who was in charge of discipline in our family and never let us get away with anything. My father, on the other hand, was very soft. He may also be the reason I've written books on masculine spirituality and why I feel very comfortable with the image of God as a father.

As you can see, what's at stake here is not so much theology as the question: how does God come to each one of us? Sometimes God must come as a friend and at other times as a lover; at other times it may be good if God comes as a father. But if you continue on your spiritual journey, I promise you that sometimes God will reveal himself in feminine form: himself as herself. And for some of us that may be the first time that we fall in love with God.

Many people, I find, don't love God at all — maybe even most people, even very many religious people. To my surprise I've discovered that many religious men and women even hate God. Naturally they can't admit that to themselves. How many people are afraid of God, how many experience God as cold and absent, how many people have a sense of God as someone who might toy with them or undercut them? They have nothing to be afraid of. All we have to lose is that false image that doesn't serve us, that image of ourselves that's always too small and that image of God that's likewise too small. We need to ask God to teach us to let go.

After my meanderings, I invariably come back to the image of Mary. Her response says it perfectly. It is all about being empty and teachable, with a "beginner's mind" that is ready to let go of what her own theology told her about God. I can see why some teachers called Mary "the touch-stone of orthodoxy." How she did it is how all humanity must do it: enlightenment or salvation is not something we do; it is something that is done to us when we become empty and free.

No monotheistic Jewish girl at that time could ever have been prepared for the Incarnation. God is perfectly tran-scendent and beyond everything. And if she believed the rabbis' teaching that God comes in words, in the Torah and in the Commandments, then nothing prepared her for believing that God could become flesh and body.

The Incarnation had nothing to do with theology. It was rather about vulnerability, about letting go, about empti-ness, about self-surrender — and none of that is in the head. It was a woman who said yes, so that Jesus could come into the world. And the more the Church gets out of its head and into its feminine soul, the more, I believe, it will become able to conceive Christ and carry him to term for the world. Not a Christ to fight over as Catholics or Prot-estants, as liberals or conservatives, but simply a Christ we can meet, a Christ we can stumble on, a Christ who won't let people "know" him, only love him.

Balancing the Masculine

The liturgical texts are almost completely patriarchal, and they perpetuate this narrow image of God. I've heard that this is even more difficult in German than in other lan-guages. In the U.S. many books have been rewritten by nuns in a new, nonsexist, and inclusive language. In our

Franciscan community we've placed great value on that. Many people think it's unimportant, but language is very important because it establishes the categories we use to interpret our experience. There are certain words that I call "sexually charged" because there's a lot of power in them. For example, the words "father" and "mother" are sexually charged, whereas the word "parent" is neutral and flat. If we said, "my parent," there would be no energy behind it. In English we try to avoid the word "men" when we're talking about people.

The structures are also unequivocally patriarchal. In Catholicism the structure is patriarchal; in Protestantism the thought models are very masculine: the pulpit in the center. Obviously a kind of balance could be struck if the rational and the nonrational, the left and the right halves of the brain, were given equal rights: an altar and a pulpit in the center of a circle. Again, a clear example is the Twelve Step program, because it's an image of the "Church from below." I believe that, regardless of our denomination, we'll make progress only by doing what we have to do. But don't leave the Church and don't let yourselves be thrown out either. Our work has to be done in a creative tension with history and with our ancestors. That's the only way that we'll finally influence history.

We belong to the first generation of the Church that has come to consciously recognize our partriarchal and sexist biases. It has been a painful and humiliating experience. I like to say that as a Church we've grown a year per century, as far as our readiness for Christ goes. That means that by now we're twenty years old. We're now beginning to pose adult questions to the Bible.

Many questions of the Reformation were asked by male clerics fighting with other male clerics. They were questions for teenagers: Who's right? Who has the power? Now we're twenty years old, young adults. Now we're ready to learn how to meet one another and love one another. As you do that, the history of the Church unfolds. But don't drop tradition: it's mothered us and fathered us, till we got to the point we are at now. We carry its burden, but we also carry its freedom. Despite all our burdens, the question of women's insight is arising above all on the soil of Western Christianity.

The Benefits of Theology versus Spirituality

Good theology is important. If I hadn't received good theology, I wouldn't have the authority to write this. But at the same time I'd like to stress how important spirituality is above everything else. And once again I'd like to reiterate that religion is one of the surest ways to avoid faith and to avoid God. That was demonstrated to us in the New Testament by the murder of Jesus. It was the priests and theologians who killed Jesus. The ones who accepted him were the lepers, the drunkards, and the prostitutes. Truth isn't where we suppose. As Jesus says, be prepared for the surprise that "the first will be last, and the last will be first." (Matt. 19:30)

The Existence of the Devil

As a student I asked my professor if the Adversary, the devil, was merely a projection. And he answered that it would really be very hard simply to shove aside the whole Bible, all of tradition, and all world religions, which generally seem to assume that there are personal evil spirits in the world. Many Indians in New Mexico, where I live, have no doubt at all that the devil exists. They even carry out exorcisms over the areas where we build atomic weapons. In our cerebral theology we're not so sure that there is a devil. But we go out and build the atom bombs. There are two extremes: either to take the devil seriously, or simply deny his existence. Personally I've witnessed too much evil to simply deny the existence of such a presence in the world.

2

Community Life
as a Challenge

❦

I WAS THE FOUNDER and (for fourteen years) the pastor of a community in Ohio.[7] In 1996 I had a wonderful contemplative year. After that I headed off to New Mexico, where I've founded a new center. Our center in Albuquerque is not so much a community as a training center for people who work with the poor and oppressed. We try to bring together concerns with spirituality and with social justice.

Around the beginning of the 1970s I was very busy with the "community of communities" (a network of American base communities). Whenever I talk about this with Jim Wallis, one of the founder/pastors of the Sojourners community and magazine, we both find it very painful, and we wonder why so many communities started up and then folded.

The most plausible answer I've found so far is that they tortured themselves to death. But I also think they had a hard time integrating spirituality and commitment to social justice issues. Some of them developed too much into "therapeutic communities" and imploded. After two or three years many members asked themselves, "What am I still doing here?" Many of the once politically oriented communities attracted a crowd of idealists, and then wore each other out with their idealism. Often they were more in love with their own ideals than with reality. If people haven't gone on a serious spiritual journey it's easy to predict that they'll be more in love with the idea of community than with the real thing.

I keep saying to new groups that it's very important to be extremely honest from the beginning about the real expectations and presuppositions that you bring with you. Of course it takes a long time to discover what these are, especially because so many of these communities have been founded by young people. In a culture like ours, where people grow up very slowly, the communities undeniably turned into places where you worked out your identity problems.

The same thing, of course, is true today about the preparation for religious life. The novice masters of religious orders have to grapple with an immense fluctuation in numbers. It's very hard to hold on to twenty-year-olds who are just then becoming adults. It's also difficult because many young people simply use these communities to grow up. But if we take the capitalistic nature of our culture into consideration, this can scarcely surprise us. Nowadays most things are looked on simply as means of expanding or enriching one's own ego. Thus community too can easily become one consumer item alongside others; and once consumed, naturally it can be left behind. Unfortunately the same rule holds at times even for marriage.

Society no longer supports the fundamental assumptions that earlier created long-term, stable community. For example, we religious have taken solemn vows, but people find it increasingly hard to understand that. This definitely holds true for celibacy, less for poverty. More and more people acknowledge the need to lead a simple life. In the Reagan era, or "yuppie" era, greed became acceptable in polite society. There is new appreciation for serving others instead of merely pursuing your own career. Many missionaries come back and tell us what's going on in the base communities of Central and South America. We're convinced that the North American Church will be converted by the Central and South American Church.

When a person is on a serious inner journey to his or her own powerlessness and is also in immediate contact with the powerless men and women of the world, then community will result.

After I had been engaged for fourteen years in a community of committed members, I deliberately wanted to do something different in New Mexico. Our main intention was not to found a community, but to gather people who had a vision of service to the world, to train them and make them qualified for this work. We were confident that, in so doing, another kind of community would come into existence as a by-product. Now, after several years we're very happy with the results. We notice that we're looking in the same direction and that in the process we're joining hands, because it's necessary — and almost accidental. We don't agonize so much about *how* to join hands. Many of our communities have, as I said, worried themselves to death, because every morning they kept sticking the thermometer in their mouths to take the community's temperature.

I really believe that the Gospel calls the whole world to a kind of community, to the possibility of a life that can be shared. But community is an art form, and there are obviously many possible ways of coming together. I know many religious who live in monasteries but who don't have the capacity for community life: they're too imprisoned in themselves. And at the same time I know many nuns who live alone in apartments but are totally community-oriented, bound up and interconnected with the lives of many people. The secret lies in the way you let other people get through to you, and the way you move out of yourself. This is, of course, at once the mystery of spirituality and the mystery of vulnerability and powerlessness. When a person is on a serious inner journey to his or her own powerlessness and is also in immediate contact with the powerless men and women of the world, then community will result.

If one of the two is lacking, people won't be community-oriented. Without an interior life and what we call "love of justice" most communities just serve themselves. We have to look out for this particularly in our country, because we're by nature rather narcissistic. We've had the leisure to contemplate our belly buttons. Because so many families break up, many people naturally enter communities to experience there the family they never had. That's understandable, but I'm convinced that people also have to be called to a vision outside themselves. Up to a certain point, even if not totally, we get healed and liberated despite ourselves — as a by-product. We can't spend our whole life working primarily to heal ourselves, because that comes by grace — it's a gift. This doesn't mean that we shouldn't take the time to work at our problems, but I believe the therapeutic society has its limits.

The Way of Life in Our Center

The metaphor that stands behind our whole center is that of a school for prophets. True, it's not written over our front door, but it's what some people call us. It's my wish (and I hope this is good Franciscan theology) to remain in the Church, but at the same time to be as far out on the edge of the Church as possible. Fortunately many bishops and religious superiors have supported me. Thus we were given the possibility of making a place where people could be trained for creative criticism — but on the foundation of faith. It's interesting that we've encouraged all the charisms in the Church — except the charism for prophecy.

The people come to us for so-called practicums, which last between two weeks and two months. And all year long we run retreats, seminars, workshops, etc. The people write to us beforehand and we try to develop an individual program based on their needs.

The essential thing about such programs is always the immediate contact with the poor and oppressed, for example, the imprisoned, the homeless, refugees or battered women. In the afternoon and evening, group work and instruction are held in the center, followed by discussion. Every participant has a mentor and a personal spiritual guide who helps him or her to digest what's going on. The crucial points of instruction lie in the realm of liberation theology, i.e., reading the Bible through the eyes of the

Third World or of women instead of through the eyes of clerics.

We stress contemplative prayer a great deal, because we feel that we're already too full of words and we've argued too long about rituals. Of course the Catholic Church demands that the eucharistic celebration be led by a priest. That's why we Catholics are afraid of forms of prayer that make priests superfluous as spiritual leaders. We need forms of prayer that free us from fixating on our own egos and from identifying with our own thoughts and feelings. We have to learn to become spiritually empty. And I see nothing apart from contemplative prayer with the power to accomplish that. This is something that we're absolutely clear about, more than anything else, and it has already yielded very good spiritual fruit.

Every day in the center begins with a twenty-minute contemplative "session": we sit and keep silence. We also teach social analysis at the center. Americans are inclined to be pretty naive: we think somebody is either an American or a communist. Fortunately that's changed somewhat now, because we can no longer simply label the Russians as enemies. So we try to give people a more accurate analysis of society, to help them interpret events in the world. Our conclusion isn't left or right, but rather the option for the poor. If you begin to analyze things intellectually, you always find truth on both sides. But we think the Gospel has given us a clear directive to stand on the side of those who are the victims. We call this the "bias toward the bottom."

I give a long course called "The Spirituality of Subtraction," in which I've tried to bring psychology, theology, and politics under one roof, and to acknowledge how we have to let go in all realms of life. Particularly as Westerners, we don't have practice in letting go. Even the churches, I think, have taught a spirituality of addition and not subtraction, a one-sided endeavor to get proofs of grace and to achieve salvation. I always thought the Protestants had reformed us Catholics in this area, but I've come to believe they're just as bad. We're all capitalists, and we've expounded the Gospel from the perspective of our capitalistic assumptions, which always leave the ego in the center and make everything into a consumer product. It's amazing how quickly a spirituality of subtraction becomes evident to people. I believe we're in the process of recognizing our shadow side, our addiction to *addition.*

Becoming Powerless

You don't make up your mind to become powerless. If you deliberately set your sights on it, that will only strengthen your own ego. We can't convert ourselves; we get converted. We have to settle in the world in such a way that circumstances, reality, can get at us. If we're all white Anglo-Saxon Catholics with the same education and biases, no one gets converted, and everybody legitimizes everybody else in whatever stage of "nonconversion" each one is in.

Ekklesia really means "those who have been called out." But we didn't get called out, we got called in. On Good Friday one year we set up stations of the cross through the whole city. We began in front of the court house (where "Jesus is condemned to death"), and then went to the prison (where "Jesus falls for the first time"). The idea of doing the stations of the cross as a political act was picked up by the people in all the churches with great enthusiasm — except for some clerics who told us, "You're pulling the people out of the Church." As if the Church had to take place in the church building. But that assumption is centuries old and very hard to overcome. This would be an example of where the Church has to begin letting go.

But the most important thing for us is to teach contemplative prayer. In the initial classes, I have to provide the participants with lots of exercises to do, to bring home to them that they shouldn't identify with their thoughts and feelings. Many of our Christian forms of prayer involve thinking about God or having feelings about God. I believe both of these forms are extremely limited. Their appeal is understandable because we localize the Gospel in the left side of the brain, where rational thinking is dominant. The left side of the brain seeks to understand and explain everything. It's afraid of entering the "cloud of unknowing."

That's the weakness of theology as long as it's separated from spirituality. For this reason we teach more spirituality than theology; historically it was the other way around. So we probably also have to let go of our need for a clear and comforting theology, because we're being led into mystery. In the final analysis that's why we have to let go of our need to keep everything under control. Most of us are very shocked to discover how great this need is.

In my opinion there are three primary things that we have to let go of. First is the compulsion to be successful. Second is the compulsion to be right — even, and especially, to be theologically right. That's an ego trip, and because of this need churches have split in half, with both parties prisoners of their own egos. Finally there is the compulsion to be powerful, to have everything under control. I'm convinced that these are the three demons Jesus faced in the wilderness. And so long as we haven't looked these three demons in the face, we should presume that they're still in charge. The demons have to be called by name, clearly, concretely, and practically, spelling out just how imperious and self-righteous we are. This is the first lesson in the spirituality of subtraction.

That lesson has many social and political implications and leads us to letting go of our political mythologies — for example, that we're the best country in the world, as many Americans believe. Pretty soon we've got to overcome nationalism. We also have to give up the compulsion to possess so many things and to have our own private stock of everything. The fact that not every one of us needs our own auto or washing machine would naturally make a good argument for physical community.

My Preferred Form of Contemplative Prayer

The most important form of contemplative prayer for us is a kind of *prayer of centering*. This form was taught very forcefully in America by the Trappists, and I learned it from them. Seen from the outside it almost looks like a Zen prayer form, because we're not trying to strengthen the ego. It's not followed by any common prayer. That doesn't mean that common prayer isn't in order; we practice it in other places. But we discovered that every morning we knew there would be community prayer we wound up reflecting on how to formulate something beautiful. As soon as prayer becomes any kind of performance or we need to critique ourselves for our formulations, we have lost the purity and directness of prayer. Also, we generally don't attach any importance to social activities like drinking coffee or tea afterward; there are other opportunities for that. So these prayer meetings don't offer any sort of reward, either social or ego-related. There's also no beautiful music playing to manipulate feelings, so the world of feeling is not rewarded. You just sit there in silence.

One of the most solid forms of "church" spreading in our country today is groups like "Contemplative Outreach" spearheaded by the Trappist Fr. Thomas Keating and the "World Community for Christian Meditation" led by the teachings of Benedictines John Main and Laurence Freeman. They are both offering a marvelously simple and yet disciplined form of "centering prayer" where the usual issues of ritual, leadership, and verbiage are all avoided by going straight to the experience of prayer itself — the substance instead of our usual preoccupation with forms. They simply let go of their ego so God can take over. If you are filled with yourself, there is no room for another, and certainly not God. I think these groups have a lot to teach us, especially in the Western churches.

Dealing with Our Fears of Letting Go

I don't advise trying to master fears. You can't fix the soul. You can only acknowledge your own rage and your fear of trusting and refuse to identify with it. Because we've lost the art of detachment, we're now an addictive society.

When I was a Franciscan novice, we learned a great deal about this distancing, but in the last twenty years we've not been talking about it in my order any more. As a result we're tied down to things. Unless we learn to let go of our feelings, we don't have the feelings, the feelings have us.

We have to ask: who is the "I" that has these feelings? The spiritual journey leads us back to this "I." But most men and women in the West have never encountered it. Instead they've become identified with their stream of consciousness, with their feelings. Don't misunderstand me: I'm not saying that you should suppress and deny your feelings. I'm challenging you to name them, identify them, and observe them. But don't fight them and don't identify with them. Teaching this art is teaching contemplative prayer in its first stages.

Now you might ask: "What does this have to do with God? I thought prayer was supposed to be talking to God or searching for God. You seem to be saying that prayer is first of all about me and getting myself out of the way?" That is exactly what I am saying. God is already present. God's Spirit is dwelling within you. You cannot search for what you already have. You cannot talk God into "coming" into you by longer and more urgent prayers. All you can do is become quieter, smaller, and less filled with your own self and its flurry of ideas and feelings. Then God will be obvious in the very now of things. It is so simple that it is actually hard to teach.

Bring your emotions and your mistrust to the Lord as an act of personal powerlessness. Say: "God, I can't not be enraged, I can't trust!" That's your emptiness. In other words, name your rage and admit it, but don't identify with it or let it identify with you. This is a great freedom that, in my view, links good psychology with good spirituality.

How Training Leads to Political Work

I've already mentioned that all our trainees have a mentor and a spiritual advisor. We have no predetermined goal as to political work for the trainees. The mentors and the spiritual advisors together with the people in question work out what it is they can concretely do when they return home. The only "prejudice" that we have and permit — after all, we're not neutral, and we've indulged in the illusion of being neutral all too long — is that we want to help the people find a place alongside the powerless. They will be their teachers, and this viewpoint will keep changing them. I don't know why it took so long for us to see that. For me this is the only way the Gospel makes sense.

This is not primarily a political position, but it can become a political position, as we can see from the example of Central America. I've been told that there have been more martyrs there in the last twenty years than in first two centuries of the Roman Church — simply because they were on the side of the poor (which is probably where the early Church was too!). At this moment two of our people are "companioning" the people in El Salvador, because the government there has considerable inhibitions about killing Americans, since we're giving them a million dollars a day. Some of us at the center have already been in jail. We're strongly convinced that forms of civil disobedience and nonviolent resistance are necessary. But we don't tell the people when and where and how they should do it. We just teach them a process for listening.

Two of the three atomic laboratories in America are in New Mexico: Los Alamos, where the atomic bomb was invented, and Kirkland, right in the city of Albuquerque. Every Friday morning we stand at the gates where eighteen thousand workers pour in to work, and we hold up posters presenting questions of faith. We try not to be self-righteous or accusatory; we simply raise issues. Fortunately this has led to a highly respectful dialogue with the people who work there; as far as I know, it's the only such dialogue in the country. We prefer this approach, namely, first posing questions and then inviting people to dialogue, although the pointed prophetic finger has its justification and its place.

Acceptance of Our Work by Secular and Church Authorities

Although I've been outspoken and critical of the Church, I'm one of the most accepted retreat masters in our country. That surprises me. Why do they invite me? I think and hope that they know I'm a son of the Church, that I don't stand outside it. I think they trust me and believe that my theology is solid, and that I don't voice criticism irresponsibly for its own sake. Positive and negative criticisms have a different energy and personality. I think St. Francis and Franciscan spirituality have taught me a great deal about how one is reformed from within.

When I was still a very young priest, Archbishop Joseph Bernardin of Cincinnati took me under his wing. He knew I needed both guidance and protection just as Francis had his "cardinal protector" when he was trying to found his new community. He knew that I would be perceived as "on the edge," but he also trusted, thank God, that I was actually "in the middle." He had a wonderful ability to distinguish between core dogmatic truth and necessary pastoral practice. He could distinguish, it seems to me, between form and substance, which is actually rather rare in the Church. I think that is one reason he has made such an impact, but also why he was hated by the far Right. His core insights on the search for common ground, the "seamless garment" of respect for life from womb to tomb, his ability to critique his own country on issues of militarism and materialism, and his personal forgiveness of enemies all shouted loudly: "true Gospel."

The Significance of Denominational Affiliation

We call ourselves Catholic ecumenists. About 70 percent of the people who come to us are in fact Catholic, but that's connected with the fact that in our region Catholics have more of a social conscience on the issues. The other 30 percent come from all other confessions. The Mennonites and Quakers are very appreciative and simply can't believe that we're Catholic. They say, "You talk like we do!"

But even in many theological training centers in the country it turns out that historical denominational differences are becoming less and less significant. We even call that "the European question" and wonder why we saddle ourselves with the historical issues.

Those people who have pressed forward to the question of *justice* have discovered that you can work with another person all day long without knowing what denomination that person belongs to. Once you've crossed the line to the perspective of justice, you find yourself looking at your denomination and your traditions quite differently. There's a surprising level of agreement on goals and less arguing about formulations of belief.

Older Communities Must Learn from the New

There are already grounds for hope in the fact that many men and women who live in older, more rigid communities are beginning to ask what can be learned from the new communities. I find the same humility and openness to such issues among many American sisters. In our country the nuns are even playing the leading role. In my child-hood we always imagined the sisters as harmless, pious creatures. And now nobody is stronger than the sisters, be-cause they're the only ones who have lived real community and who have reciprocally educated one another in the process. Their missionaries came back and opened their eyes to the poor. Of course, within the Church they were in the position of the oppressed, vis-à-vis the clergy. And so they had, as they have now, an advantage over the priests, who are continually forced to maintain the status quo.

The sisters sometimes develop very creative forms of community, and they're even ready, if need be, to give up their canonical status. When they do, a surprisingly large number of them notice that their communities originally had no canonical status at all — in other words they weren't recognized by the Church — and that often their foundresses hadn't even intended to attain that status. They're content to be lay women who live in community. These communities increasingly include married couples and single people who haven't taken a vow of celibacy. This may be compared to what originally was the "Third Order."

I believe you've got to trust your own experience and your own heart, and take risks. I think there will always be a form of celibate life in the Church; it has historically borne too much fruit for it not to continue. But it's obviously not the only possible mode of community life. In our center I'm the only one with a vow of celibacy. All the others are married or single people without vows. It's a lay movement. I repeat: we place no special emphasis on community in the formal sense or as an end in itself. It's a by-product of people heading in the same direction.

The Difference between Sound Therapy and Incarnation

The problems of the spirit can't be resolved with the brain. We have to move in the direction of a more body-related therapy and in the process give more weight to the right half of the brain. We also have to find forms of therapy more oriented to action. We named our center the "center for action and contemplation," deliberately putting action first. We learn and are healed by committing ourselves.

Yet this is an act of faith for which we can show no proof. Self-oriented persons would prefer not to believe this. They always want to go rummaging about in their own souls. It's hard to get people across this borderline.

I recall the early days of New Jerusalem: there were many people who were strongly influenced by the charismatic movement. They were possessed by the idea of getting healed, and they constantly refused to be there for others, because they first had to become whole themselves. Once they were whole, they'd help others. I'm not exaggerating: to this day these people are still not healed and they're still waiting. Their narcissism prevents them from ever being healed. In the last fifteen years we've often replaced spirituality with therapy. We have to see the limits of the therapeutic society without denying its positive gift. Good psychology has nothing we need to be afraid of.

The Role of the Priest in Prayer

I feel it is important for us to guard against too many rituals. I hope we're living in a world where there's a both-and. This means that if we want to correct an imbalance, we don't immediately have to fall into the other extreme. Most people at our center say that the monthly eucharistic celebration is now, as it has been, our most important get-together. While we gather daily in the center for contemplative prayer, we hold a Eucharist only once a month. I think these services are very beautiful, because many different gifts come into play there. We don't deny the role of the priest in them, but neither do we glorify it. In Greek, liturgy means "the work of the people."

We don't need pyramids; we need circles. Pyramids don't create community; circles do. The same is true for the priest. He too needs a place where he can be a brother like all the others. After over thirty years as a retreat master I know that priests themselves do not flourish inside of a system where they are always on top and always on display. It is rather toxic for their own soul and their own development as human beings. When you are always a projection screen for everybody else's God issues, it becomes very hard to handle your own alternating inflation and deflation. Too many priests burn out on either end, trying to live up to grandiose expectations or unfairly hating themselves because they know that they are naked underneath their vestments like everybody else.

The Future of New Jerusalem

As a founder of a community, one has a wonderful but in some ways negative influence: you're able to hold a community together almost despite yourself. By staying for fourteen years at New Jerusalem (the community I founded), I put off the necessity of forming a lay leadership that came from the group itself. After I left they endured many painful years. The people had to decide: What do we really want? And not just: What does Richard want? They chose three very good lay pastors. And they carried out some very prophetic actions: the community's first house, where I lived after we moved into that part of the city, was placed at the disposal of refugees from Central America. So I believe they're finding their way and their direction again. But dark times are among the best teachers.

3

Getting Rid of the Church

❧

MY THOUGHTS ON THE SUBJECT of the Church are offered in the context of who and what I am: a man
of the Church, a Franciscan; I'm a priest and I'll die as one,
unless they throw me out first.[8] So my words will come, as
it were, "from inside the family" and not from outside.

I would like to begin discussing the Church with the
largest image possible: creation. I start with creation because it's God's primary revelation, as Paul says in the
Letter to the Romans: "Ever since the creation of the world
his invisible nature, namely, his eternal power and deity,
has been clearly perceived in the things that have been
made." (Rom. 1:20) Even though we can't see God, we
can discover God in what God has created. This is what
we mean by a "theology of creation": we start not with
the problems that came up later but with what God created. In the last verse of the first chapter in the Bible
it says: "And God saw everything that God had made,
and behold it was very good." (Gen. 1:31) This is the
only time in the whole Bible that anything is called "very
good." But we've been so focused on the later problem
of redemption that we've forgotten what God said in the
very beginning. We are so trapped in our own tiny moment that we forget the big picture. And I assume God
understands this.

There was once a TV program called "Life on Earth" in which the whole history of creation was telescoped into a year. The earth began in January. Around April the reptiles first made their appearance. In September came the mammals. I don't remember all the intermediary stages, but I know that humans came very late. *Homo sapiens,* the "wise man" as we like to style ourselves, emerged in the last three minutes of December 31. That means that the whole Judeo-Christian tradition was played out in the final milliseconds of December 31.

I find it hard to believe that God was speaking for the first time in those final milliseconds. St. Bonaventure called the creation "God's fingerprint." We've forgotten to study this fingerprint because we're so busy with our theological theories.

Jesus invites us as the Church to become a new community of human beings; he calls us a little flock. I don't believe he ever wanted us to be the whole — only the part. He said we should be the yeast, the leaven, not the whole loaf. He called us to be the salt, but we want to be the whole meal. He urged us to be the light that illumines the mountaintop, but we want to be the whole mountain. The images that Jesus uses are very modest and yet very strong. The continent of Europe had the goal of "being Christendom," and hence it's very difficult now for us to be merely leaven and salt and light. We hardly know how to do that. We want to lead; we want the way of power. We thought we had to be the whole loaf, whereas he tells us to be just the leaven. That is a much more humble, fragile, and even invisible position. It feels powerless and will appeal only to people who frankly don't need power. The rest of us will all abuse and misuse the Gospel for our own purposes, and that is, unfortunately, much of our history.

When Jesus described this new reality, he obviously was *not* talking about the Church. But the Church — just like the people of Israel — has continually been tempted to idolize itself. Yet if it adores itself, it can't adore the One who alone deserves to be adored. The proclamation of the Reign of God means that only *one* thing is absolute — everything else is relative. Everything else is merely a means to the end. That includes the Church, the Bible, the sacraments, and all the exercises of spiritual life. None of these is an end in itself. As the Zen masters say, they are not the moon but the finger that points to the moon. But we spend most of our time arguing over who has the best finger and who has the true finger, instead of looking to the moon. This is quite clearly a transgression of the First Commandment, namely, the forbidding of the worship of idols.

The first image of an idol was made by the first priest, Aaron. As soon as Moses came down from the mountain, glowing from the experience of the mystery, his brother Aaron quickly introduced religion by making the golden calf. By creating idols, we have God at our disposal, we have God in hand, we're in control. The temptation of religion always consists in turning the tables so that we ourselves take charge of the situation. Thus the first mistake consists in confusing the Reign of God with the Church.

The second and more frequent mistake consists in confusing the Reign of God with heaven, as if we enter into God's Reign, or Kingdom, only when we die. But Jesus' prayer makes it quite clear: the Kingdom of God is here, "Thy Kingdom come." It's not here in the sense that we can grab hold of it. "If anyone says to you, 'Lo, here is the Christ,' or 'There he is!' do not believe it." (Matt. 24:23) It will never be so bound up with any institution or reality that we can be in control. The Reign of God is never going to be coterminous with any one anything, and God can operate however and wherever God wants. There will not necessarily be a signboard out front with the word "Christian" on it. This is very humbling for institutional religion to recognize, but also very necessary. As Jesus said, "Not everyone who says to me, 'Lord, Lord,' shall enter the kingdom of heaven, but he who does the will of my Father who is in heaven." (Matt. 7:21)

Four hundred years later St. Augustine said: "Many belong to the Church who do not belong to God. And many belong to God who do not belong to the Church." In our group egocentricity we confused the Church with the Reign of God. Try to think of the Reign of God as Jesus' way of saying, "The Big Picture" or "In the largest frame." It is *not a place as much as the ultimate perspective,* the perspective of God. Whenever you open yourself to the Big Frame your little frame of reference shrinks into proper perspective or even falls away entirely. As I like to say, "When God's kingdom comes, your kingdom goes."

Jesus' harshest words are aimed at hypocrites, and the second harshest at the people who are primarily concerned with possessions. He says that power, prestige, and possessions are the three things that prevent us from recognizing and receiving the Reign of God. When he says that to good, upright people, they react with indignation and consider his remarks scandalous. They call him an unbeliever, an enemy of the law, and finally a devil—because they *own* too many things that they now must defend. The only ones who can accept the proclamation of the Reign are those who have nothing to protect, not their own self-image or their reputation, their possessions, their theology, their principles, or their certitudes. And these are called "the poor," *anawim* in Hebrew. In the Magnificat, Mary sums up the spirituality of the *anawim*.

If in this world we are already living in the reality of the Reign of God, then the world becomes relative and we become "pilgrims and strangers." Life can't be based on the passing; it can't be based on transitory images. Instead, we know we have to base it on the truth, on the truth of who we are, on the truth of this creation, which God says is "very good."

Our problem consists in the fact that we're so convinced of *not* being good. And we need a great deal of trust to believe God's pronouncement that everything God created is very good. We seem to believe that only perfect things are lovable. Yet the Gospels say very clearly that God loves imperfect things. But it's only the imperfect and the broken who can believe that. Thus it happens that God throws a party — and the "good" people don't come. That's why God says that the cripples, the lame, and the blind are to be invited — and they would be ready.

This pattern has never changed. Those who don't have anything to prove or protect can believe that they are loved as they are. But we who have spent our lives ascending the spiritual ladder have a harder time hearing the truth. For the truth isn't found up at the top, but down at the bottom. And by trying to climb the ladder we miss Christ, who comes *down* through the Incarnation. I'm convinced that many of the guilt feelings that haunt the middle class, much of its widespread poor self-image as we call it, and much of its self-hatred and self-centeredness are due to the fact that we have settled into a world that Jesus says we should never be at home in. If you base your life on illusion, you will naturally hate yourself. The proclamation of the Reign of Heaven is the most radical political and theological statement that could ever be made. It has nothing to do with being perfect. It has to do with living inside of the Big Frame, the final and full state of affairs, the lasting perspective. It is not a matter of thinking differently or attending a particular kind of church service or living with a new kind of theology of redemption. We don't think our way into a new life; we live our way into a new kind of thinking. The Gospel is before all else a call to *live* differently, so that life can be shared with others. In other words, the Gospel is ultimately calling us to a stance of simplicity, vulnerability, dialogue, powerlessness, and humility. These are the only virtues that make communion and community and intimacy possible.

I believe that the religion of the middle class was always tempted to use Scripture primarily to dispense consolation. But the Word of God, like a mirror, must first *confront* us with ourselves. Second, it has to *challenge* us to live in a new way, to lead a life of authentic brotherliness and sisterliness — economically, politically, socially, and spiritually. Only after the Word of God has confronted and challenged us do we have the right to take *consolation* from the Word of God as well. But we've drawn consolation from the Bible before we changed our lives! The Christian nations are among the greediest and the most intent on security of any in the world, while they maintain that Jesus is their Lord and their security.

I've had the opportunity to preach in many parts of the world. A non-Christian once told me: "Why should we believe in your Christ? You Christians have waged the most wars, you use up the most resources in the world, and you've raped the planet. And then you say you love your poor Jesus. You hate Jesus and only say you love him to fool yourselves." I have no response to this, because I know I am not innocent either. Over large parts of this planet Christianity and the Church have dwindling credibility. If we're honest, we have to admit that we've turned them into theories of redemption and psychic trips. For us the Gospel has never really landed on earth; it's never touched the sociopolitical and economic order; the Kingdom of God never came. False religion is present when we piously say, "Thy Kingdom come," but don't immediately add, "My kingdom go." And we Christians have believed that we could both say, "Jesus is Lord!" and go on being the lords of our own lives.

We say, "Jesus is Lord!" and still believe, as Americans do, that we are the most significant nation in the world. That sort of Gospel isn't credible, and neither is that sort of Church.

I'm convinced that we've been so busy worshiping the messenger that we have ignored the message. The greatest part of the Sermon on the Mount has never been taken seriously — neither by Catholics nor by Protestants. All of us have to be reformed. But I believe that we're little people; God is too big for us. We're just about to become adults, to honestly let the Gospel speak to us, to listen to what

Jesus says, in no uncertain terms, about poverty and about leading a simple life in this world, a life that shows trust in God and not in our own power and weapons. And yet, we're now spending 60 percent of our resources to "protect" ourselves, although God never promised us security in this world. God promised us only truth and freedom in our hearts. But we didn't want the Reign of God, we didn't want the "Pax Christi." We wanted the "Pax Romana"; we wanted triumphal Christianity.

If in this world we are already living in the reality of the Reign of God, then the world becomes relative and we become "pilgrims and strangers." Life can't be based on the passing; it can't be based on transitory images. Instead, we know we have to base it on the truth, on the truth of who we are, on the truth of this creation, which God says is "very good."

What does all this mean for us? It means that we're on the way. It does no good to hate ourselves. We stand on the shoulders of our forebears and carry the burden of their sins and the fame of their holiness. They are an image of what we are, and we are an image of what they were. As you head out on the inner journey of faith, you will discover that you are exactly the same as them: you will find many things in yourself that you're afraid of and that you don't like — if you're really honest. But if you remain on the way, you will also find a part of yourself that you know is very good; you will discover *who you are in God.* You don't earn that; it's what you are. This is a net that cannot fail you.

To preach the Reign of God, dear brothers and sisters, we have to break with our *dependency on* a perfectible self. People who have suffered, people who are twisted out of shape, people who are oppressed have a lead on us. Those of us who are good, sound, and strong have a hard time getting out of the starting blocks.

If you suffer and are confronted by limitations, you know that reality isn't perfect. You sense this from below, from your gut and not just from your head. Your trust is not in "progress" but in mercy.

Several years ago I heard the following story: William Casey, the head of the CIA, had just died. He was a good Irish Catholic, and his good Irish wife was on TV that evening. Around that time the newspapers had already begun to discover a lot of corruption in the CIA. Mrs. Casey said that anyone who raised questions about her dear husband was committing "blasphemy." As a good Irish Catholic, she surely must have known the definition of blasphemy. Blasphemy doesn't mean defaming the CIA, but defaming God. But when a country makes itself God, then it can't hear the Gospel. We use Christ to prop up our own nation-state, and then we use the Church to bless the nation-state and its illusions.

Religion and culture have been so united in most of history that we had to pay a very small price, if any, to be a believer. Actually there was a large social pay-off for being "religious." Then why does Jesus say, "The world will hate you"? (John 15:19) I have to ask — we all have to ask — "Does the world hate us?" At present, there's nothing to hate, because most of the time we Christians play the same game as all the others. We haven't built our lives on a new reality; we've built them on the same old reality as all the others: power, prestige, and possessions. The real religion of America has always been America regardless of whether one was Protestant, Catholic, or Jew. We used our own lovely phrase for it: "The American Dream."

As I have mentioned, we can't make up our minds to convert — we *get* converted. We get converted despite ourselves. We can only ask to be able to live with open hands, to become practiced and prepared in the art of letting go, so that the Gospel can teach us how to be poor in this world — with nothing to prove or protect. Jesus says it will be "good news for the poor," but not for those who have a lot to defend. (see Luke 4:18)

In large parts of the universal Church something wonderful is happening: many people are coming to hear the proclamation of the Reign of God and to commit themselves to issues of justice. And in the process we notice that the historical questions raised by the different denominations are not the important ones. The questions of the Reformation were mostly questions of educated white male clerics — and they were questions of power and justification. Who has the power and who's right? That's what adolescents argue about. But we're twenty years old now, and we're ready to listen to the more substantial questions about the Gospel, about community, about nonviolence, about loving one's enemies, about leading a poor and simple life in this world — points that Jesus expressed his opinion about quite unequivocally. His statements about the sacraments and the priesthood are much less clear.

We've never burned people as heretics for not caring about the least of their brothers and sisters, although it does say in Matthew 25 that this is the only thing we'll be judged on. For a long time I thought I'd be judged on how many Masses I'd attended. And until a few years ago I always had an irreproachable Sunday balance sheet. I thought I'd be judged on how perfect I was and how well I had kept the Ten Commandments. I was quite disappointed to discover Matthew 25, because God doesn't even mention them there. And yet I had a pretty good record that I could have shown God. God says, "Did you recognize Christ *in the least* of your brothers and sisters?" This is the only time in Scripture that the same thing is repeated four times in a row, so that we can't miss the point — and still we've managed to do just that. We come back and ask, "But when did we see you hungry and thirsty?" Evidently we don't even have to know that we're doing it for Jesus (fundamentalists beware!). We only have to do the act. In creation God has revealed what God is. And if we meet this creation in its brokenness and its poverty, we meet "Christ in his most distressing disguise," as Mother Teresa says.

I would like to offer some practical encouragement. Many of us first take the outward journey and discover outside of us a reality that's broken or poor or wretched — and in the process we learn compassion for ourselves. Many of us begin from within and are driven outward. In either case we have to go *the whole way.* If you go the whole way inward, there too you'll discover something that's broken and poor and in need of compassion. In the language of St. Francis this is called "the leper within us." Francis couldn't bear to see lepers. But he says in his Testament that as soon as he embraced the first leper what once had

been hateful to him became "sweetness and life." Many of
us first have to learn to embrace the leper within us before
we can embrace the leper outside. In the final analysis it's
the same act of compassion. And it's not a compassion
that we produce, but a compassion that's given to us.

Many of us were brought up with a totalitarian spirituality, not with a spirituality of compassion. "Kill the
enemy, attack the enemy!" was the message — and so
we've attacked and killed ourselves. But if we learn a new
spirituality of nonviolent compassion toward our own soul,
we'll have the same present to offer the world. As I mentioned, many groups outside the Church are discovering
this better than the Church itself. And that may be the
reason the churches have become so weak. We're busy
with power, while spiritual power, and many of the "little
ones" of this world have discovered powerlessness. I mentioned in particular the program of Alcoholics Anonymous
and the Twelve Step program. I believe these groups are
in many ways a model for what the mystery of the Church
could be. And the decisive first point is the radical experience of one's own powerlessness, which drives you into
a circle of men and women who share the same experience. And I believe this is the fundamental mystery of the
Church: two or three gather in his name, perhaps without saying his name at all — because his name is broken,
bleeding flesh. And if we surrender ourselves to this experience, we betake ourselves into the flesh of Christ. In
other words, Christ redeems us all despite ourselves. No
tradition and no Church will triumph before God. We all
stand in need of eternal compassion. In short, it is the two
poverties that convert us: the poor man/woman within

and the poor man/woman without. They drive toward one another.

The Meaning of Community

Living in community means living in such a way that others can access me and influence my life and that I can get "out of myself" and serve the lives of others. Community is a world where brotherliness and sisterliness are possible. By community I don't mean primarily a special kind of structure, but a network of relationships. On the whole we live in a society that's built not on community and cooperation, but on competition.

The Need for Resurgence of Base Communities

The New Testament provides an example of what can be called a house Church — a base community of probably about forty people. I've been tremendously influenced by what's happening in Central and South America and by the reciprocal relationship between the base communities there and the institutional Church. If we have only the institutional Church, everything very quickly becomes formalized or legalistic. But if we have only the base communities, then we often have just a flash in the pan. These communities are normally successful for a short time, but history has shown us that they quickly become narrow and sectarian. I'm convinced that we grow best when we live in a creative tension between the two types of Church and idolize neither of them. The problem is that for four hundred years we've had nothing else but the institutional Church. We didn't have permission to experiment a lot with base communities. So we have to do it now, even though we'll undoubtedly make some mistakes in the process.

In Brazil alone there are eighty to a hundred thousand base communities. That would never have happened if there had been a whole lot of priests. God had a better idea. This doesn't mean that the institutional Church is false. But something else has to bring it into equilibrium and keep it honest. I'm sure that many of you come from churches that in the beginning were on fire. But in the end every community recapitulates the whole path of conversion. That's why my advice for most people is to blossom where they were planted and to deal with realities in little groups, but also to remain connected somehow or other with the institution, because the institution will still be there after our little groups have long since passed away. At a basic level this has something to do with respect and love for our ancestors, however strange that may sound. I always have to tell Americans this because we think that we're the beginning and summation of history.

The Importance of Balance

There is a risk of becoming a purely therapeutic community that revolves around its own ego. *The act of our faith consists in donating and giving away what we don't yet have* — that's what makes it faith. This is hard for us to understand: how can I give away something that I don't even have? Nevertheless I go out and heal others, even though I myself am not yet healed. I heal them through my brokenness, not through my power! A church community that doesn't include an outwardly directed service for others, a service extending beyond itself, is simply not a Church, it's not Christ. It's psychology or false transcendence. That doesn't mean that psychology is a bad thing; it just isn't the same thing.

The Shift of the Church Center to the Third World

I suspect that the movement of church history today does not have its center in Europe. All the signs speak against it. Nowadays 70 percent of all Christians live in the Third World. Europe has had its chance on the stage. Now the Bible has to be interpreted through the eyes of women, through the eyes of the poor, and through the eyes of a communitarian picture of the world, as I've found in Africa, through a more body-centered spirituality and through a more contemplative spirituality, as you can find in Asia. This doesn't mean that we were wrong, just that there are many other parts of the mystery of Christ that have to be unveiled. And our part as traditional churches is to be humble enough to let go and to let the other voices have their say.

4

Christians and
Political Commitment

❧

ON THE LAST DAY OF THE YEAR, the feast of St. Sylvester, I generally withdraw to pray.[9] So a few years ago I asked myself: what should I pray for this year? What do we need in these turbulent times? Naturally I was strongly tempted to pray for more love. But it occurred to me that I've met so many people in the world who are already full of love and who really care for others. I believe that what we lack isn't love but wisdom. It became clear to me that I should pray above all else for wisdom in the decade to come.

We all want to love, but as a rule we don't know how to love rightly. *How* should we love so that life will really come from it? I believe that what we all need is wisdom. I'm very disappointed that we in the Church have passed on so little wisdom. Often the only thing we've taught people is to think that they're right — or that they're wrong. We've either mandated things or forbidden them. But we haven't helped people to enter upon the narrow and dangerous path of true wisdom. On this path we take the risk of making mistakes. On this path we take the risk of being wrong. That's how wisdom is gained. On the spiritual path the enemy isn't pain; it's *fear* of pain. We haven't become wise, because we're so afraid of pain.

I believe that there are two necessary paths enabling us to move toward wisdom: a radical journey inward and a radical journey outward. For far too long we've confined people to a sort of security zone, a safe midpoint. We've called them neither to a radical path inward, in other words, to contemplation, nor to a radical journey outward, that is, to commitment on the social issues of our time. We prefer to stay in a secure middle position, probably because these two great teachers, the inner and the outer way, both cause pain. Failure and falling short are the best teachers; success has practically nothing to teach on the spiritual path. But we notice that many of us incline to the one side or the other, on account of either temperament or education. Wherever I travel in the Church, I find people who focus inward and people who are activists. These two types seldom come together, and thus they both miss half the Gospel, they both lack half the truth.

I feel certain that we in the West have to begin primarily with action. The great temptation of the Western Church has been to imprison the Gospel in our heads. Up there we can be right or wrong, our position can be correct or false, but in any case everything always remains firmly in our grip. On the other hand, action never allows us the illusion of control, at least not for long.

Action is the preferred starting place for the Western extroverted personality. We don't tend to go inside first, but we tend to do, try, move, experiment, touch, and experience. Call it pragmatism if you will, but we tend to find out if things are true or false by engagement *with* them instead of thinking or theorizing *about* them. True action never

permits the delusion that we will always understand everything. The advantage to this hands-on approach to life is
that it can often serve as its own corrective, if we are willing
to learn and listen. It can keep us humble and growing and
trying again, or we can remain forever in our heads with
our utterly untested theories and theologies. The authority
of suffering and the authority of those who have suffered
has a better chance of guiding us instead of mere ivory
tower explanations. Although it sounds counter-intuitive, I
actually trust people who act a bit before they contemplate rather than folks who just keep "contemplating" and
it never seems to lead to action or engagement. I see the
same bias in Jesus and in Christianity when compared to
Buddhism or New Age teaching.

It looks as if we are condemned to live in a world that
is a mixture of darkness and light, of good and evil. Jesus
spoke of the field in which wheat and weeds grow alongside each other. We say, "Lord, shouldn't we go and rip out
the weeds?" But Jesus says: "No, if you try to do that, you'll
probably rip the wheat out along with the weeds. Let both
grow alongside each other in the field till harvest." (Matt.
13:24–30) We need a lot of patience and humility to live
with a field of both weeds and wheat in our own souls.

We'll never conquer evil if we launch a frontal assault. If
we do that we may incorporate into ourselves the energy
and the weapons of evil. We can end up turning into what
we hate.[10] That's why Jesus told us we have to love our enemies; otherwise we become just like them. Hitler is thought
to have said that the wonderful thing about Nazism was
that all those who directly attacked it became fascists themselves in the process. The U.S.A. has a lofty self-image

and thinks it conquered fascism. Nevertheless America has supported extreme right-wing regimes in Guatemala, El Salvador, and South Africa. You hardly ever see your own sin; you tend to rationalize your sin away as virtue. For this reason we need help in recognizing that we ourselves are a mixture of good and evil.

There is no perfect political system. Jesus never promised us that any political system could realize the Reign of God on earth. He advised us to take a humble position in this world, a position of nonparticipation in the lie. His metaphor for this position was "yeast." But we want to be the whole loaf.

> **I believe that there are two necessary paths enabling us to move toward wisdom: a radical journey inward and a radical journey outward. For far too long we've confined people to a sort of security zone, a safe midpoint. We've called them neither to a radical path inward, in other words, to contemplation, nor to a radical journey outward, that is, to commitment on the social issues of our time.**

It's very hard for the Church to accept a lesser position, to do our work with integrity and truthfulness and leave the future to God. There is no perfect theology, there are no perfect explanations, there is no perfect road leading to psychic health. We are forced to live in a world that contains both life and death. The Reign of God is already here, but it's not yet whole. Faith means standing in this position and holding on to paradox at the same time. If we take the contemplative path, then we see the shadow side and the inconsistency of our own souls. If we take the path outward, then we encounter the place where the victims are. If we try to get to the truth by arguing, we will find good arguments on both sides. At some point we must risk the dangerous decision for faith, which means always standing on the side of the weak, always on the side of the poor, always on the side of the victims.

As a rule, standing on this side will make us unpopular. We'll be misinterpreted by the opposite side. Remember in Central and South America there have been many martyrs. The main reason for their martyrdom was that they stood on the side of the poor. In Matthew 25 Jesus told us that we would someday be judged by whether we had stood on this side and had recognized him there in the least of our brothers and sisters. Jesus' option for the poor is a war of the Lamb. He goes down the "low road" that we're all afraid of.

The Bible presents history always from the perspective of the victims, those who were oppressed, who were enslaved, who were poor. It is a partisan presentation of history that takes the side of the disadvantaged. But we were overzealous in understanding the story from the side of the *victors!* Perhaps it means for all of us that we have to go precisely to the place where we're most afraid, ashamed, and oppressed, even to the place where we hate ourselves. Only in that place can we establish the connection between the path inward and the path outward. If we learn to acknowledge and love the poor man and the poor woman in our own soul, we'll understand the truth that is hidden in the poor man and in the poor woman whom we find outside ourselves.

The Bible speaks of four forms of poverty: there is first the poverty of sin, the poverty *before conversion.* In this condition the person is completely empty and missing the truth. For such people the word of God is, "Repent and live!"

The second poverty is the poverty of *oppressed men and women,* who have no time or the means of living in a way truly befitting their humanity (for example, the enslaved and abused Israelites in Egypt). And here the word of God issued to Moses is, "Change the situation!" The whole Judeo-Christian tradition begins with God's command to change history, to oppose the pharaoh. Nevertheless God requires the Israelites to wander through the wilderness for forty years and to endure a process of purification. Here we see the very first connection between the inner journey and the outer journey.

The third poverty the Bible speaks of is the poverty of a *simple and humble life.* It is the challenge of living simply, of placing our hope and our trust in God and in other people instead of in material things. Because we never learned to take that seriously, in either the Catholic or the Protestant tradition, we have fallen prey to the totalitarian systems of this century that always *force* us to do what Jesus *asks* us to do freely. Communism tries to enforce equality, Nazism tries to enforce security and solidarity within a group, fundamentalist religion tries to shame and psychologically coerce people into an "only way." The biblical God seems to just call us to simplicity and patience, which keeps us outside of every totalitarian big system or overarching explanation. It looks as if God always takes the risk of freedom: God too demands, but then God simply waits. God waits as long as necessary until we can love of our own free will. God is not only modest, God is also very patient. The political systems of this world have no patience.

The fourth poverty in the Bible is the deep realization of our own limitedness and weakness. This is the central motif of the Sermon on the Mount: "Blessed are the poor in spirit. Blessed are those who weep." (Matt. 5:3ff.) Many things in life cannot be changed; we can only grieve over them. So long as we are no longer under the *compulsion* of wanting to change them, we have the *freedom* to change them. Then the change comes from much greater depth — not from our anger, but from a place of integrity; not from a place where fear dwells, but from deep trust; not from a place where self-righteousness rules, but from wisdom.

There are at least two different ways to be a prophet. The first is the way that Moses took. His task was to tell enslaved men and women: "You can be free!" The second way is the way of Jesus. To men and women who consider themselves free he says that they are actually enslaved. The second way is much rarer and much harder. Today we may need both kinds of prophets.

The Gospel says we aren't really free so long as we haven't been freed from ourselves. And no political system can teach us or offer us this freedom. When Mother Teresa came to America, she called us one of the most unfree peoples in the world. We Americans are paralyzed by all our possibilities. We consider ourselves a tremendous nation because we can choose from a gigantic menu of consumer articles. Even Christians are ready to believe this sort of nonsense. When they do, they avoid traveling through the depths of the wilderness. Again, our enemy isn't pain, but the fear of pain.

Jesus came to teach us the way of wisdom. He brought us a message that offers to liberate us from both the lies of the world and the lies that are lodged in ourselves. The words of the Gospel create an alternative consciousness, solid ground on which we can really stand, free from every social order and from every mythology. Jesus called this new foundation the Reign of God. And he said the Reign of God is something that takes place in this world and yet will never be completed in this world. This means that we're back where we started: with faith. We understand now why Jesus keeps asking: "When the Son of man comes, will he find faith on earth?" (Luke 18:8) It is so rare to find ourselves trusting not in the systems of this world or any system, but standing at a place of both light and darkness, at a place where we offer our salt, our leaven, our light on the mountain. But we have no security that we're really right. This means that we have to stand at an inconspicuous, mysterious place, which seems more dark than light: "When the Son of man comes, will he find faith on earth?" At the place of faith I'm not sure that I'm sure.

Jesus never promised us security in this world, and yet we're ready to buy any political system that promises us quick and easy security, instead of living in this essential insecurity, in this deep inner poverty, where we really grow in wisdom. It's in the school of the victims that we learn something, not the school of the winners, not the school of security.

That is why, dear brothers and sisters, I believe that we Christians are steadily becoming a smaller group. There are simply fewer and fewer reasons to be Christian on social grounds. For centuries the churches have held the nation-state system together and strengthened it. Christians have often failed to get to a place that wasn't dependent on rulers, dictators, and kings. This is an anxious situation. Without the light of Christ and without faith in the presence of God none of us would want to stand there. "When the Son of man comes, will he find faith on earth?" It's beautiful that in spite of everything we can still give voice to these words in the Church, and that you're ready to lend an ear to such a crazy truth. This shows me that the Church is still a place of hope, that we can preach the folly of the cross.

A Jewish master once said: "God is not nice. God is not an uncle. God is an earthquake." We've created a "bourgeois" version of Christianity that has manufactured a nice God. We want Jesus finally to take away our insecurity. We want to feel as if we are just wheat and not weeds. But God isn't nice, and God isn't an uncle. God is an earthquake. In a way the preaching of the Gospel pulls the rug out from under us. We have to put our life on a new footing. I believe we've always thought that we could reason our way into the Gospel. But we'll never solve the way to a new life in our heads; we have to live our way into a new kind of thinking. First we have to act. We have to dare to cross over this threshold and live differently so that, starting out from this point, we can again ask challenging questions. That's why action and decision come *first*.

To get a real grasp of the truth of the Gospel, I believe we have to enter into solidarity with at least one person who's different from us. This means crossing over the line to the other side. For example, if you're afraid of a certain race or a certain religion, then the best thing is to head directly there. If a certain set of people scare you, then you have to enter into solidarity with them. We have to endure being with those people for a while and learn to view reality from their standpoint. That's why Jesus says we have to love our enemies. It's the only way to grasp the whole picture. It's the only way to learn to love the other side of our soul.

But I repeat: don't try to solve it in your head; simply act. From the vantage point of this action you'll understand what I mean. The problem isn't solved in the head but in the gut, in the whole body (including the head, but that doesn't come till later). And that's what I mean when I speak of the risk and the leap of faith. This is a very Franciscan approach to life. St. Bonaventure and Duns Scotus put love as prior to knowledge, probably building on Francis's own headlong dive into life. First you agree to give yourself, and then you will understand it, not the other way around. Otherwise you get caught in all kinds of protective reasons why you do not need to give yourself and you never make the dive.

First I have to act, and then I'll understand — meaning the whole person will understand. Then I'll know what I know. But I really won't know *why* I know. I also won't be able to prove to you why I know something; it's the mysterious wisdom of faith. It's the wisdom you learn only when you're on the way. This is a lesson nobody else can teach you, neither the pope nor biblical authorities; you have to go down this road yourself. That's what the "primacy of action" means. Persist at that deeper place in yourself where the "both-and" is located. This is the place of the soul, the place of wisdom, toward which we have to move. Don't be afraid! Fear comes from a need to control. And we are not in control anyway.

The Compulsion to Be Right

Jesus' commandment isn't, "You shall be right," but "You shall love one another." Of course, it's not necessarily wrong to be right on an issue. The problem begins when we face an inner compulsion always to be the ones who are right. If we're too taken up with this question, then we're continually absorbed with our self-image, and such people were precisely the ones who killed Jesus. This is an eternal pattern: the moral high-ground, that is, the same compulsion to be right and powerful that killed Jesus! Here we have to make a very delicate distinction: naturally we should be obedient to God, but we're not supposed to maintain our positive self-image at any price (and sometimes that looks very much like obedience). The genuine saints of every age were unconcerned with their own holiness and didn't consider themselves saints.

I have a rule of thumb that says that those who believe they are holy aren't. Jesus said that the prostitutes, the tax-collectors, and the sinners would enter the Reign of God rather than those who sit before him in the synagogue. When Jesus healed sick people, he always said: "Your faith has made you whole." He never said, "Your correct doctrine, your orthodoxy, your dogmatism have healed you."

I too hope, of course, that I'm acting correctly, but I can't continually circle around this question. The problem is precisely in the *need* to be right and the *need to think of myself as right.* That is the problem for the soul. I have to do my work and leave the judgment to God. I need to avoid the compulsion to be constantly passing judgment, because those constantly passing judgment are not in a position to honestly perceive their own reality.

Naturally we have to learn to distinguish between darkness and light. But we dare not succumb to the illusion that we ourselves don't have a share in the darkness. The darkness we see is always a part of us. We can't naively skip over the subject of darkness and light. And it's precisely because we were so naive that we so often became victims of dark powers and called them light. I tell people who want to be prophets: you can't play the prophet until you've discovered in yourself what you accuse others of.

The Renunciation of Being Right

I believe we have to commit ourselves to the path to which God has called us. And we have to go all the way along that path. Those of us who have met Christ have to let him lead us all the way. I personally believe that Jesus represents most perfectly the heart and nature of God. But the Second Vatican Council says that Jesus is the light and the truth but that other religions also "reflect a ray of that Truth which enlightens all." (*Nostra Aetate,* 3) A "ray of Truth" had best be respected and received, and I would much sooner have that light than the darkness of arrogance and pride.

The absolutely crucial thing is to "go deep in one place" and let your God lead you to a place of surrender, love, and humility. Until then you do not understand or love your God anyway. The paradox is that when you make an "exclusive" commitment to "Jesus as your personal Lord and Saviour" (to use the recent language of many groups), you are in fact committed to inclusivity! *Because he was!* That is the seeming contradiction that most fundamentalists never resolve.

I personally believe that we rather totally missed Jesus' major point when we made a religion out of him instead of realizing he was giving us a message of simple humanity, vulnerability, and nonviolence that was necessary for the reform of all religions — and for the survival of humanity. We need to dedicate our lives to building bridges and paying the price in our bodies for this ministry of reconciliation. (Eph. 2:13–18) The price is that you will always, like all bridges, be walked on from both sides. Reconcilers are normally "crucified," the "whole world hates them," because they are neither on one side or the other, but building the vulnerable bridge in between, which always looks like abdication of ground to the "true believer."

Jesus is a person and at the same time a process. Jesus is the Son of God, but at the same time he is "the Way." He's the goal, but he's also the means, and the means is always the way of the cross.

For all Eastern teachers, their message is the same as their life, or their life is their message. For some reason, we want the "person" of Jesus as our "God totem," but we really do not want his message of "descent" except as a very functional message — this is what Jesus did to save us. We do not want it as a pattern of life and a path of our own liberation.

The way of the cross looks like a way of failure. In fact, you could say that Christianity is about how to lose and win, how to let go creatively, how the only real ascent is a true descent. We need to be concerned with following Jesus, which he told us to do seventeen times, and less with worshiping Jesus — which he never once told us to do.

The Dangers of Dogmatism

Most of the crimes in this world have been committed by people who thought they were right. Thomas Aquinas says, "All people chose something that seems good to them." We all believe we're right. I'm sure the Nazis imagined *they* were in the right, and the comrades of the SED [Sozialistische Einheitspartei Deustchlands] imagined they were in the right. That's why we have to set off on an inner spiritual path that finally shatters the illusion of a world that breaks down into black and white. The way inward demands that you build bridges with your own soul. But anyone who builds a bridge always runs the danger of being trampled from both sides, of being misunderstood by both sides. Like the prophets we ourselves stand "in the breach," and like them we run the danger of going under.

I've never found that a lot of wisdom comes through people who have planted themselves dogmatically somewhere or other. I have found that a great deal of wisdom comes into the world through people who creatively hold the tension of opposites on difficult and complex issues. Their outstretched arms, nailed in the truth on both sides, make them look like the crucified, who was a living icon of the opposites of human and divine, heaven and earth, male body and female soul, hanging between the good thief and the bad thief, which is the two parts of all of us. That is a magnificent image of transformation. The First Commandment says that we're not to worship idols. Idols are attempts at explanations that give us the feeling of being absolutely right, and then we adore these explanations. Our justice (and this is good Lutheran theology) is always a gift of God and not of our own doing. That gift is given to us mostly despite ourselves. But the gift is not bestowed if we continually ask, "Am I right? Am I right?" Faith doesn't always allow us such quick comfort.

God as an Earthquake

Let me say once more that people who have had strong emotional experiences of God must also dare to step out into the world. The God who has touched them is leading them to do the same. We become like the God we adore. A dogmatic person has a dogmatic God. A compassionate person has experienced the compassion of God. A God who actively engages with you leads you to the same kind of active engagement with others. Basically how we do relationship with God is how we do relationship with others, and how we do relationship with others is probably the most honest indicator of how we relate to God. Relationships seem to be the "earthquakes" that shake our ground and lead us to new places, both when we do them right and more commonly when we do them wrong. Those are the teaching moments. They lead people who are socially and politically active into an inner world where there is nothing to "do" and where they no longer have everything under control.

The farther we go on the journey of faith, the more faith has to do with trust and self-surrender. The Kingdom of God leaves none of us in our own little kingdom where we decide what happens. God leads us all, like Abraham, out into a new country.

Moving Away from a
Cerebral Comprehension of God

The longer I preach the Gospel on all five continents, the clearer it becomes to me that Europeans feel most at ease in their heads. I first got a real awareness of this in Asia and Africa. Africans feel comfortable in their bodies, and I believe that this is just as legitimate a way to Christ as our "head way." It is no surprise that so many Asian-based religions try to get you to center in the solar plexus (or the gut), and their martial arts try to teach you to move from that place. This is also a very good way to get in touch with the Divine Indwelling. Latin Americans are often localized in the heart. I tease my Mexican friends that I have never heard a song from their country that does not have the word *corazón* somewhere in the lyrics. They laugh with recognition.

People from these cultures are showing us that in the future the Gospel will be expounded more from the perspective of the body, the heart, or the gut, and less from the head. That doesn't mean that our approach has been wrong. I repeat: the question is not whether we were right or wrong. But this development shows that we're only a part of the whole.

The Christian Church is finally becoming a universal, global Church. I hope in the coming of the cosmic Christ, a Christ whom we comprehend not just in cerebral categories. Back home in New Mexico the Indians dance on their feast days from morning to night. And they ask: "Why isn't this just as good as your praying with your mouth?" I know they're right, of course. And when I see the fruits of their life, I sometimes have the impression that they're "righter" than we are.

The Place of Feelings in Faith

Most of us need an emotional experience just to get out of the starting blocks. Precisely because our faith was up in our heads for so long, many of us have to experience the love of God emotionally. Many people have had this experience in the charismatic movement. Feelings are admittedly a good point of departure, but not a good means of continuing to grow spiritually.

I'd like to compare it to a marriage. You can't stretch out the honeymoon forever. If we try to prolong the honeymoon, then we're not in love with a person, but with an idea, with an ideal image. All the great believers that I know are people who surely have moments now and again when they've found deep emotional consolation. But they don't need these moments — and they don't continually seek them. Feelings are a very good thing, but please don't make an idol out of them or believe that religion means producing the maximum amount of good feelings. If you do, you remain very immature.

Many of us have been taught to repress negative feelings. We should allow, feel, and observe our feelings — including the negative ones. Negative feelings have the power to open us up to parts of ourselves that are still afraid and not able to trust. As long as we haven't become aware of these feelings, we can't open ourselves to God; we don't even know who we are. Sometimes we also have to say to God: I'm afraid, or I'm furious, or I feel rejected. Some of the great prayers of all time demonstrated a freedom to get furious with God. Job is an example of this.

The Challenge and Opportunity in Marriage

The reason I think almost all people are called to marriage is that we need another person to be like a mirror for us, to reflect our best self and our worst self. The interesting thing about a mirror is that it doesn't change the image; it simply takes it as it is. We all need the experience of being loved unconditionally. Without a human experience of unconditional love, which we hope to experience in marriage, we can't believe in God's unconditional love. And this is obviously the case, because to go the whole way with God, we must at the same time go the whole way with another person, though often that's very difficult. For this person always shows us our dark side and reminds us that we still haven't really *learned to love*.

5

Contemplation —
the Spiritual Challenge

❦

I DON'T BELIEVE THAT JESUS had a plan of what the perfect society was supposed to look like.[11] In any case this plan isn't evident from the New Testament. Instead, Jesus gave us a process, a way of hearing, a way of union, a way enabling us to look past the world of appearances and to press forward to the truth. To be free and empty of oneself, free not to make an idol of any system, is real freedom that makes community possible.

Let's take that journey into emptiness one step further. I call this the journey into contemplation.

We live in a society that places great importance upon external signs of success and importance. We have to assure ourselves and others that we are valuable and important. I see us in contrast to the Pueblo Indians that we Franciscans work with in New Mexico. They actually "downplay" status or any external sign of superiority. The outside of each house always needs to look ordinary and even a bit ramshackle. They wear common and ordinary clothes, and on the feast days uniform clothing is worn. This is the way they maintain community and avoid comparison and competition. It is no surprise that the Spanish invaders named them the "pueblo" or "community" Indians. We, however, place great importance on the distinctiveness of our cars, clothes, and dwellings. We tend to be preoccupied with being "one up" on others. We have great difficulty finding our value from within. In a materialistic society we have projected our sense of worth almost exclusively onto things. That is why it's hard to rediscover our souls in ourselves.

People living under capitalism find it very hard to know their own center and to live from within it. We live in an affluent society that's always expecting more, wanting more, and believes it has more coming to it. But the more we own, ironically enough, the less we enjoy. This is the paradox that lies within all material goods. The more we project our soul's longing onto things, the more things disappoint us. Happiness is an inside job, and when we expect to find it outside of ourselves, it is always a disappointment. We then seek a "higher" or more stimulating experience and the spiral of addiction increases. As the alcoholics say, "You need more and more of what does not work." Now they have even coined a word for it, "affluenza," the addiction to money and status symbols that seems to have no limits.

In America we possess many things that we call time-saving conveniences, and yet we still run around and never have enough time. In an affluent society where the soul's longing is projected outward, we have much more information, but much less wisdom. Wisdom comes from dealing rightly with the information, but information has become a consumer item in its own right. We have no place deep inside us to integrate this information and transform it into wisdom. Hence our social system may produce many specialists, but very few wise men and women. And in the end we're short of knowledge, wisdom, and time.

When the soul is projected outward, we have less time for love, because we turn other people into articles for consumption too. We keep asking only: What can this person do for me? How can the other be useful to me? How can this person enrich my own self-image? How can he or she contribute to making me feel still stronger? That's why there are so few experiences of genuine friendship that's grounded in itself, with no goal above and beyond the relationship.

It's also no surprise that we no longer have any notion of the spiritual life, because even God has become a consumer item. There are bumper stickers with the slogan, "I found it," with the "it" supposedly meaning God. But actually the "I" stays in the center: *I* found it. Even God has become a possession of my ego.

Ultimately we do the same thing to our own souls: we stand, as it were, outside ourselves and pass judgment on ourselves. Are we valuable or aren't we? Are we right or wrong? But as we judge ourselves, we also tear ourselves apart. We separate ourselves into the part that passes judgment and the part that gets judged. We have to find a way to bring those pieces back together again. The only way I know is the way of contemplation, which is counter to the way of capitalism.

Jesus quite definitely wanted us to build a society in which people come before things. Jesus taught us to love people and to use things. But in our society we use people and love things. Some years ago I was preaching in Africa, in the cathedral of Nairobi. The people listened to me for hours, and at the end I was invited to pray with them. They gathered in the sanctuary and sat down on the floor. An old black man prayed, "Lord, never let us move into stone houses." And I nodded and said, "Yes, Lord," though I had no idea what this prayer actually meant. The praying lasted more than an hour. Then I went into the sacristy and asked the priest why the man had said this prayer. The priest answered, "You know our country. People here live in little huts, and huts have no doors. That's why your family is my family, and my family is your family. The only family is the extended family. But as soon as you move into a stone house, you build a door. And on the door you put a lock. And behind this door you begin to collect your belongings, and then you have to spend the rest of your life defending those belongings." Thus the world is divided for all time into "mine" and "thine."

Over eight hundred years ago Francis of Assisi said exactly the same thing: we own nothing; we're owned by our possessions. I believe this is unavoidable unless we find the place for our soul. If we don't live from within our own center, then we'll go spinning around things. The true goal of all religions is to lead us back to the place where everything is one, to the experience of radical unity with all of humanity and hence to the experience of unity with God. Religion has no other purpose than to make possible this one journey. And this is just what I'd like to describe in somewhat greater detail. But I have to say right off that it's quite difficult to describe this journey with words. For the crucial point is that it's *your* personal journey, a journey that you have to take yourself.

Some years ago my Franciscan superiors gave me a year's leave to spend in contemplation. I know it was a great privilege, and it struck me as a luxury. As a motto for this "sabbatical" I chose the maxim of the Austrian philosopher Ludwig Wittgenstein: "Don't think, Just look." I decided to fast from books, radio, and TV, so as not to take in any more information and ideas. I wanted to try to get a good clear look at what I had already experienced and lived until then. I didn't need any fresh information; I had to learn to reflect upon previous experiences, to chew them thoroughly. I had to taste on my tongue their positive and their negative sides, their sweetness and their bitterness.

I had previously given a retreat for a Trappist monastery, where the abbot asked me whether he could do me a favor. I asked him to allow me to live for thirty days in the hermitage of the famous poet-monk Thomas Merton, who died in 1968. I had read the books of Thomas Merton — who was also the teacher of Ernesto Cardenal — and was very enthusiastic about him; he was my model. I thought that if I were at his place, I might be able to absorb some of his wisdom. And so I managed to spend the spring in the hills of Kentucky, absolutely alone with myself, with the woods, and, I hoped, with God. I thought beforehand that it would probably be deadly boring. I wondered what I'd do all day long. I put my chair in front of the door and watched the sun come up in the morning. And in the late afternoon I placed my chair on the other side of the hut and watched the sun go down.

That doesn't sound especially edifying. I tried to keep a diary of what was happening to me. Because I'm a man and because I'm of German extraction, I find it particularly hard to cry. But one evening I laid my finger on my cheek and found to my surprise that it was wet. I wondered what those tears meant. What was I crying for? I wasn't consciously sad at all or consciously happy. I noticed at this moment that behind it all there was a joy, deeper than any private joy. It was a joy in the face of the beauty of being, a joy at all the wonderful and lovable people I had already met in my life. Cosmic or spiritual joy is something you participate in; it comes from elsewhere and flows through you, and it has little or nothing to do with things going well in your own life at that moment. Thus the saints would rejoice in the midst of suffering, which to the rest of us is unthinkable.

But at the same moment I experienced exactly the opposite emotion. I hadn't known that two such contrary feelings could coexist. The tears were at the same time tears of an immense sadness – a sadness at what we're doing to the earth, sadness at the people whom I have already hurt in my life, and a sadness too at my own emptiness and stupidity. And even today, years after this experience, I still don't know whether joy or pain had the upper hand – they lay so close to each other.

In this year of contemplation I wasn't preaching or teaching anything. I wasn't capable of verbally transmitting my inner truth, and that's why it had to come out of my eyes instead of out of my mouth. There is another way of knowing reality besides the merely cerebral. We can know with our body, our intuition, and now we have scientific evidence that the heart does "know" real information. We are moving toward a more integral understanding of knowing, and that is what contemplation seeks. It will not be perceived, however, as information as much as groundedness, peace, inner clarity, assurance, and even an unexplainable enthusiasm. Thus contemplation feels like a kind of knowing that the saints called "unknowing." They describe it as an encounter with the "cloud of unknowing," where we are no longer governed by the compulsive need for security, where we no longer have to understand everything, where we can say from the depths of our heart: "It's all right" – although at the same time we know that much is not all right, that many things in the world are terrible. And nevertheless we find the inner strength to live with reality as it really is.

The best definition I know for contemplation is as follows: *Contemplation is a long, loving look at what really is.* The essential element in this experience is time. There is a qualitative difference between ten minutes and ten hours, and even more, of course, between ten hours and ten days. We have to find a place where we can receive all our experiences without repressing anything. We need a place where there's room to consider everything that we've done – and not done – in our life, a place that's bigger than Yes or No, a place bigger than the judgments that we pass. At this all-embracing place God becomes quite clear. Here there is room for every part of you and for God's presence.

Some years ago I gave a Bible course on the subject of redemption. We went through the whole Bible and looked at how the theme of redemption, of salvation, unfolds. The first presentation of salvation is found in God's promise to the people of Israel. God promises to give them a spacious country to enfold them. When we had completed the whole Bible, we could find no better description of redemption than this first one: God promises us a spacious place within – and that's the place we call the soul. We don't *save* our soul; we *discover* it. We don't go there and try to make ourselves holy; we wake our souls up. We're already united with God; the problem is, we don't believe it.

Thus the central issue is always trust. It is "allowing" God to give Himself to me apart from being worthy of it. As wonderful and unbelievable as that it, it is also very humiliating for the egoself. Thus the natural temptation is to find methods to make ourselves "worthy." It is almost the only way that the capitalist mind can understand reality at all. We make everything into buying and selling. We naturally operate by "the performance principle." We can't believe that we're loved with nothing in exchange, absolutely nothing. Our real value depends on what we are and not what we do. We continually try to be good people, whatever that means. In reality we are not always *good,* but we are *holy.* Being good is something that we earn or acquire or achieve, but we're holy because we came forth from God. That's just a fact.

Contemplation means returning to this deep source. Each one of us has to try to find the spiritual exercise that helps us to come to this source. If reading the Bible helps you, then read the Bible. If the Eucharist helps, then celebrate the Eucharist. If praying the rosary helps, pray the rosary. If sitting in silence helps, just sit there and keep silence. But we must find a way to get to the place where everything is. We have to take this long, loving look at reality, where we don't judge and we simply receive.

Most of us have lived our whole life with a steady stream of consciousness, with a continual flow of ideas, images, and feelings. And at every moment of our lives we cling to such ideas or feelings: I don't have the idea; the idea has me. I don't have a feeling; the feeling has me. We have to discover who this *I* really is, the one who has these feelings or these thoughts. Who are we ourselves — behind our thoughts and feelings?

> **The true goal of all religions is to lead us back to the place where everything is one, to the experience of radical unity with all of humanity and hence to the experience of unity with God. Religion has no other purpose than to make possible this one journey.**

I'm sure that most people in the Western world have never really met the person who they themselves really are. Because at every moment, all our life long, we identify ourselves either with our thoughts, our self-image, or our feelings. We have to find a way to get behind our thoughts, feelings, and self-image. We have to discover the face that we already had before we were born. We have to find out who we were all along in God before we did anything right or wrong. This is the first goal of contemplation.

I ask you to imagine a river or stream. You're sitting on the bank of this river, where boats and ships are sailing past. While the stream flows past your inner eye, I ask you to name each one of these vessels. For example, one of the boats could be called "my anxiety about tomorrow." Or along comes the ship "objections to my husband," or the boat "Oh, I don't do that well." Every judgment that you pass is one of those boats. Take the time to give each one of them a name, and then let it move on.

For some people this is a very difficult exercise, because we're used to jumping aboard the boats immediately. As soon as we own a boat, and identify with it, it picks up energy. But what we have to practice is un-possessing, letting go. With every idea, with every image that comes into our head we say, "No, I'm not that; I don't need that; that's not me." Again and again we have to tell ourselves this. Some of the boats that are accustomed to our jumping aboard them immediately think we just didn't see them the first time. That's why they head back upstream and return. The boat says: "But before this he always used to get mad at his wife. Why didn't he this time?" Some of you will feel the need to torpedo your boats. But don't attack them. Don't hate them or condemn them: this is also an exercise in nonviolence. You aren't allowed to hate your soul. The point is to recognize things and to say, "That's not necessary; I don't need that." But do it very amiably. If we learn to handle our own souls tenderly and lovingly, then we'll be able to carry this same loving wisdom into the world outside.

Many of us have come to know only a totalitarian spirituality. For this reason it's also no surprise that we have produced two totalitarian worldviews: capitalism and communism. Both are lies. We have to learn the truth, not in our head, but in our soul, at the place where great freedom is, where God is patient and accepts everything, and where we must learn to accept everything too. At the same time, we aren't allowed to remain stuck to anything. This is also an exercise in letting go. Positive thoughts are just as bad as negative thoughts, positive feelings are just as bad as negative feelings — if we get attached to them. Positive self-images are just as addictive as negative self-images — if we cling to them. That's why Jesus says: blessed are the poor in spirit. The poor are the ones without any image of themselves to hang on to. They don't punish themselves with negative images, but neither do they continually have to protect positive self-images.

Psychology can only help us to arrange our images somewhat differently, to get a somewhat more positive image of ourselves. But authentic spirituality not only shifts the images, it says, "I don't need any images at all; I don't have to protect any self-image." If you see this exercise through, in a short time you'll know which images you personally cling to, which patterns of thought energize you. I warn you, it's a humiliating experience at first, because most people will find out that they don't know who they are apart from their thoughts and feelings. But after only a few minutes some will find that the river is cleared of boats. Occasionally it even happens that people have the feeling that they'd love to tear their clothes off and dive into the river. The water is our spiritual self that flows much deeper than our psyche.

St. Bonaventure says, "Being and goodness are one and the same thing." That's why we have to return to the level where we simply "are," where we're naked, and where we experience how inherently good we are, and yet paradoxically that goodness has nothing to do with my own performance. It is a total unearned gift. We have to return to this place; otherwise there will never be any radical

reformation of religion, nor will there be any truly new politics. There will only be one ego warring against another.
An ego with a right-wing ideology is just as bad as an ego
with a left-wing ideology. A capitalist ego is just as bad as
a communist ego. Genuine religion leads us beyond these
egocentric attitudes and helps us to see who we are in
God. There we have the freedom to be poor and ordinary.
We don't have to prove anything, we don't have to defend
anything, and we return from this place to the world with
greater strength. Indeed we're flung back into the world.

After my sabbatical year I found my way to the conviction that I should open the Center for Action and
Contemplation in New Mexico to help people to get thoroughly involved in the issues and goals of social justice, to
help people turn to the poor, but from the right point of
departure – because you can do the right thing for wrong
reasons. For this reason I ask you now simply to sit in silence for six minutes. With this exercise there's no such
thing as success or failure. The important thing is to see
it through and to keep letting go of the unnecessary false
self – and not to be afraid.

Because being and goodness are identical. The goal of
all spirituality is that in the end the naked person stands
before the naked God. The important thing is that we're
naked. As you know, the act of lovemaking requires naked-
ness. And the same is true with loving God. We have to
cast off our false self to be ready for real unity with God.

Don't be afraid of the silence, because God is with you
and leading you in that holy silence.

After the exercise you should take a few minutes' and try
to find a word, an adjective, a phrase for what happened

to you during these six minutes. (Again, "false" or "correct" does not apply here.) Even if it frightened you, or if you had the feeling that you couldn't do it, write it down. And if it was wonderful and peaceful, then write that down.

Contemplation is a way to hear with the Spirit and not with the head. Contemplation is the search for a wide-open space. This space is broad enough for the head, the heart, the feelings, the gut, the subconscious, our memories, our intuitions, our whole body. We need a holistic place for hearing. As Christians we have to go to this place if we're looking for wisdom. If we don't produce any more wise men and women, then the reason is that we have forgotten the art of contemplation.

The Effect of Contemplation on Daily Life

Of course, we have to return to our "boats," but we can't have any genuine freedom unless we know who we are apart from them. In the final analysis the purpose of letting go is so that we can freely lay hold of something. And the purpose of this new liberation from bondage is so I can commit myself from free and healthy motives. The effect of contemplation is authentic action, and if contemplation doesn't lead to genuine action, then it remains only navel-gazing and self-preoccupation.

But I'm convinced that if you stick with it, if you do this exercise regularly, then you will come to the inner place of compassion. In this place you'll notice how much the suffering of the world is your suffering, and how committed you are to this world, not cerebrally, but from the much deeper perspective of your soul. At this point you're in-destructible, because there you find the peace that the world cannot give. You don't need to win anymore; *you just need to do what you have to do,* as simplistic and naïve as that might sound. That's why Augustine could make such an outrageous statement as "love God and do what you want"! People who are living from a truly God-centered place instead of a self-centered place are dangerously free precisely because they are tethered at the center.

But you can't solve the problem by just acting "in-teriorly" or from correct inner motives. I also suggest committing oneself in solidarity to a person who is differ-ent from you, for example, to an old person, a handicapped person, a retarded person, a homosexual, or a person on welfare. If we view reality from the standpoint of others, then we'll experience complete conversion, namely, inner *and* outer transformation. We will have "turned around," and that is the biblical meaning of metanoia.

Becoming Empty

On the way to contemplation we do the same thing that Jesus Christ did in the wilderness. Jesus teaches us not to say, "Lord, Lord," but to do the will of his Father. What must primarily concern us is that we do what Jesus has bidden us do. Jesus went into the wilderness, ate nothing for forty days, and made himself empty. Another image of that emptiness is the body of Mary. She can receive Jesus into that emptiness and bear Christ to the world because she is his poor handmaid.

Of course, emptiness in and of itself isn't enough. The point of emptiness is to get ourselves out of the way so that Christ can fill us up. As soon as we're empty, there's a place for Christ, because only then are we in any sense ready to recognize and accept Christ as the totally other, who is not me. All I've taught here are the first stages, the fundamentals. Jesus takes it from there!

Discerning God's Spirit at Work in Us

Our goal consists in doing the will of the Father in heaven. Thus we first have to remove our attachment to our own will, so that we can recognize the difference between the two. Throughout history, many people who did horrible things were unshakably convinced that they were doing the will of God. That's why we have to find an instrument to distinguish between God and us. Paul calls this the gift of discernment of spirits. We have to learn when my own spirit is at work and when the Spirit of God is at work. This exercise is only a very rudimentary little step toward contemplation. I'm sure there are a thousand further steps.

I'd like to encourage you to keep on going. If this exercise teaches you nothing, then please try something else. The only person who prays well is the one who prays often. The only success (if we can talk about success in this context) is in sticking to it, in hanging on. With emptiness we are, so to speak, cultivating fertile soil where we can be receptive to the seed of God's word. Once again, I don't believe that Jesus dumps the harvest into our lap. He shows us a process of growth. He shows us a way we can learn to hear God. He shows us a way we can forgive. He shows us a way of self-surrender. He trusts that his people, as they go along this way, will learn to hear the truth ever more clearly. The great truth will always lie beyond us. The great truth will never underpin a small world.

The most convincing social activists in our country were and are at the same time people of prayer: men and women like Dorothy Day, Martin Luther King Jr., or Jim Wallis. It's very important that we bring the contemplatives and the activists together in the Church. Because neither is credible without the other. Both incorporate only a half of Christ. Christ went into the wilderness for forty days; only after that did he begin to preach the Reign of God and to heal the sick. And along the way he kept saying to his disciples: "Come, let us withdraw and find a quiet, peaceful place." (see Matt. 14:23)

This means that the Christian life must be a constant journey back and forth between the radical way inward and the radical way outward. We all begin either on one side or the other. That's why we all have to be converted to come to the place where they meet. It's the path of the true Church and the way of Christ.

6

The Freedom
of the Sons and Daughters
# of God

❧

IN MY BOOK *The Wild Man,* I tried to describe how men can be liberated. In *The Naked God,* I spoke about how the Church might be freer.[12] In *Discovering the Enneagram,* Andreas Ebert and I describe how individual men and women can become free.

The world isn't capable of recognizing genuine freedom or of making it possible. It doesn't even have the tools for the job. Besides, the world necessarily operates on the basis of particular interests, and so private egoism is simply extended through group egoism.

For me this is exactly the situation that we have to deal with: How can we, as men and women of the Church, really be liberated? How can we pass on this freedom to the world? I would like to clarify this question on the basis of a story (from Luke 8) about a miraculous cure.

> Then they arrived at the country of the Gerasenes, which is opposite Galilee. And as he stepped out on land, there met him a man from the city who had demons; for a long time he had worn no clothes, and he lived not in a house but among the tombs.

This is a picture of a man who lives among the dead and isn't quite civilized, because he runs around naked. We shall soon see that the city is comfortable with the fact that this man lives out there — and so is he. Because when Jesus comes to him, we are told:

> When he saw Jesus, he cried out and fell down before him, and said in a loud voice: "What have you to do with me, Jesus, Son of the Most High God? I beseech you, do not torment me."

The man did not know whether he wanted what Jesus had. His unfreedom was the only world he knew.

We feel much more comfortable with our slavery than with freedom. Freedom means that we have to assume radical responsibility for what we are. To be enslaved means that we always have somebody else to blame for our problems. An evil spirit had already possessed this man for a long time: "He was bound with chains and fetters." In this way people tried to keep him under control. Although they kept him chained, they said the evil spirit was holding him captive. When we project the darkness in us onto another person or other groups, then these people or groups end up accepting our projection. Sooner or later we all believe the world's version of who we are.

Hitherto we've always tried to realize freedom as the liberation of specific individuals. But Western Christianity has for the most part neglected to address the problem of institutional evil and structural sin. Christianity has often not recognized that in a great number of cases such evil is the primary cause of our individual lack of freedom. And we shall see how true that is, if we go on reading the story.

"Jesus then asked him, 'What is your name?' and he said, 'Legion.' " This means that evil has many faces, and it's hard to give it a concrete name. It's very hard to pigeonhole this evil, because many demons had entered the man, and he had been told many lies.

> And the demons begged him not to command him to depart into the abyss. Now a large herd of swine was feeding there on the hillside; and they begged him to let them enter these.[13]

The herd of swine typified the economy of this region: the people of this region made their living by raising pigs.

> So he gave them leave. Then the demons came out of the man and entered the swine, and the herd rushed down the steep bank into the lake and were drowned. When the herdsmen saw what had happened, they fled, and told it in the city and the country. Then the people went out to see what had happened, and they came to Jesus, and found the man from whom the demons had gone, sitting at the feet of Jesus, clothed, and in his right mind.

You would expect the next line to say, "And they all rejoiced," or "They were very happy." But verse 35 says, "and they were afraid."

In our work with alcoholic families we often find that the whole family dances around the person with the illness and gets upset about how terrible the alcoholic is and how hard family life is because of that person. But as soon as the alcoholic decides to get healthy, nobody gets more agitated about it than this family. Because now they no longer have anyone to shame or blame; now they have to grow up themselves. We call this co-dependency. We reciprocally bind one another with our lies; we bind one another through our negative feelings and our negative ways of thinking. And this holds true not just for families, but also for churches, for institutions, and for countries. Moving away from this trap always brings a terrible amount of anxiety. That's why, for example, Jesus says something that we've never understood. He says we must dare to hate "father and mother and brother and sister." (Luke 14:26) Preachers hesitate to give a sermon on this text because we don't know how to handle it. He says that the family and society can be a source of death, just as they can be a source of life.

The eyewitnesses report how this man was healed. And then the whole crowd of people from the region of Gerasa begs Jesus to leave their territory. The whole city says in effect: "Get out of here; you've ruined our economy. Our pigs are dearer to us than salvation, because our pigs are our source of income. We can't imagine that our economy also ruins us; our economic system is our salvation, not you."

The practical definition of freedom that we have formed under capitalism is to have endless possibilities and options. But Jesus also said that we should expect no freedom from the world. The freedom it offers us is always a freedom that serves its own purposes. It is a tiny freedom. It is the Pax Romana, not the Pax Christi.

"Then the man from whom the demons had gone begged that he might join him." We meet here one "born again," someone who has just experienced a healing and who would like to deepen his personal relationship with Jesus. "But Jesus sent him away, saying, 'Return to your home, and declare how much God has done for you.'" It was as if to say, "You're no longer the problem; the people in the city are! And it makes no sense at all for me to liberate people and evangelize them and send them back into sick cities, send them back into sick countries, with their supposed private salvations." Biblical salvation is the salvation of history and humanity itself and not just of separate or isolated individuals.

Individualism has taken away the credibility of the Gospel in the Western world because we think we can seek our private freedom — independently of others. But genuine evangelization must move forward on two rails. We must simultaneously evangelize individuals, calling them to freedom, *and* evangelize institutions, nations, and systems, calling them to conversion. If you do the first, you will be called a saint; if you do the second, you'll be called a communist and a revolutionary. And for this reason most of us remain safely on the first side. Few of us are ready for the full freedom of Christ. We want the freedom of Christ only so long as they don't take our "swine" away from us, and we can live comfortably "among the tombs."

Anne Wilson Schaef has published a very helpful book in which she deals with our personal addictions and dependencies; she describes Western society as a dependent society.[14] The obvious dependencies are, of course, alcohol, nicotine, coffee, and food. In America in the 1990s the so-called Twelve Step programs were doing a booming business. Everybody seemed to belong to one self-help group or another. And these groups grew five times as fast as any born-again Church. But we have discovered a second kind of addictive dependencies and call them "process addictions."

It's quite clear that the accumulation of money, the collecting and hoarding of money, is an addiction. People pile up more money than they can spend in a lifetime. Yet some of these people have the nerve to quote the Sermon on the Mount and consider themselves followers of the poor Jesus. There are also workaholism and the addiction to buying things — both process addictions. We say, "Shop till you drop." People buy things as a pastime, as recreation.

Three decades ago I was a novice in the Franciscans, and back then we were told a great deal about letting go. We were taught that less is more, and that the thing for Franciscans was to live simply in this world. For many years now, people in our order have scarcely been talking about letting go. But if you can't talk about letting go, you're already an addict. If you forget the virtue of giving away, you're already an addict.

All spirituality is about letting go; how to let go of our security, our good reputation, our identity and our self-image. All great contemplative teachers lead us in this direction. But because we no longer understand any of this, we have become an addictive society and an addictive Church. A large part of religion shows all the indications of addiction and dependency: people who are turned on by a certain kind of language in a desperate attempt to maintain their self-image, or people, for example, who need to consider themselves good or redeemed. They run to Jesus and say, "Good master," and his answer is, "Why do you call me good?" (Mark 10:8)

For Anne Wilson Schaef there is *one* addiction that over-arches all these quite private addictions and dependencies: *our addiction to the system itself.* Our chief dependency is the dependency on our hallowed explanations. Could there be a world not built on competition? We can't imagine it. Could there be a world not built on power? On money and control? On militarism? We can't imagine it — which shows how dependent we are on our systems. We have to throw the Sermon on the Mount out the window, because judged from the viewpoint of other explanations of the world we're all addicts.

In her first book, Schaef still cautiously called the system "the white male system" (which naturally prompted many furious letters from white males). That is why she says in her second book, "I no longer call it 'the white male system,' I now call it 'the addictive system.'" But it's white men who in the first instance profit from it. It's white men who in the first instance have laid down the rules for it. This system works to their advantage. And I have to say this because I am a white man. I come from a country that considers itself the best country in the world. I am of the gender that considers itself more powerful and intelligent than the opposite sex. I have spent many years going through the educational system. I am an ordained priest. That means I stand right at the top of the pyramid.

Often the thought goes through my head: how can I really understand the Gospel at all? Because the Gospel — as Francis of Assisi illustrates — is best understood when you're below and not when you're on top. I have a disadvantage in understanding the Gospel, but I am also compelled to speak, precisely because I am white,

American, male, educated, and ordained. We must unlock this whole thing from inside. If a woman got up to say the same thing, she'd be called a raging feminist. If a layman stood up, they'd say he must have had bad experiences with the clergy. If somebody from another country said it, they'd say he's just anti-American or anti-capitalistic. That's why *I* have to say it. I enjoy the fruits of the system. It was created for me and my kind.

Schaef goes on to say that the addictive system is undergirded by myths. Until we look these five myths in the eye, we haven't begun to become free from society, because we're dependent upon social props that we don't recognize or admit to.

The first myth is that there is only the male system, that our worldview is the only rational way to look at reality. All fairly intelligent and clever people think exactly this way. But the Gospel says that until we leave our own standpoint behind, we are not yet converted. It's called narcissism or cultural arrogance. The biblical word for it is "blindness." Jesus, for example, never suggests that rich people are deliberately bad or mean. He says they're merely blind; they can't see. The rich man can't see that Lazarus is eating the crumbs in front of his door. (Luke 16:19ff.) He's a charitable person, but he understands nothing of justice. The great question in the spiritual life is always the question of blindness and sight. And therefore our prayer must always be, "Lord, help me to see. Let me see where the demons really are — and what the village really loves."

The second myth maintains that this system, our way of thinking and living, is by nature superior to all other ways, and hence its rules and laws have to be binding for everyone. America, for example, wants to arm the world for democracy. And should elections not turn out to our satisfaction, then we decide on a trade embargo against the country and send money to influence the next election. And when the election works out the way we want it, then we triumphantly rejoice over the "victory of democracy."

Individualism has taken away the credibility of the Gospel in the Western world because we think we can seek our private freedom — independently of others. But genuine evangelization must move forward on two rails. We must simultaneously evangelize individuals, calling them to freedom, *and* **evangelize institutions, nations, and systems, calling them to conversion. If you do the first, you will be called a saint; if you do the second, you'll be called a communist and a revolutionary. And for this reason most of us remain safely on the first side.**

The third myth consists in thinking that our system is omniscient, that our way of thinking and living gives us the right to judge the reality of other people. White men know what the poor need. White men know what blacks need. White men know what women need. With that sort of attitude there's obviously no possibility of a turnaround and change. And that's why in this context "conversion" is understood as something very private, limited, individual, or sacramental. I can have my intimate relationship with the Lord Jesus and dispense with going back to the "village."

The fourth myth claims that because we have the truth, it's possible for us to be absolutely logical, rational, and objective. And whoever doesn't agree with us is simply not intelligent.

And that leads to the fifth and most shocking myth: if the four previous myths are true, we ourselves can be God, because we are almighty and omniscient. But if we take ourselves to be God, then we call everybody who criticizes us a devil. Never forget, dear sisters and brothers, that it was the religious people who called Jesus a "devil." (John 8:48) It wasn't the prostitutes, the alcoholics, or the tax-collectors — they didn't call him Beelzebub. It was the good, pious religious people who wanted to safeguard their self-image, who wanted to maintain their theology, who wanted to stabilize their church system.

Sometimes we clerics have the hardest time hearing the Gospel. Sometimes it's very hard for us to speak about freedom, because if you were free you would not need us. Sometimes I believe that we pastors mainly try to keep our jobs safe. We can't let you become independent of us. We clerics must finally have the courage to allow you your necessary spiritual path, with all the risks that entails for our church systems. Of course, you'll make mistakes in the process, but we've already made them anyhow. What seduces us into assuming that what we've done until now is so terrific? Choosing the path of freedom always means taking a risk-filled route. It means taking the chance of perhaps doing something wrong. There's always the risk of making mistakes. But what is a mistake? And what does a mistake on the spiritual path mean?

Success has very little to teach us in the spiritual life, but failure and fiascoes are great teachers. Continual experience of so-called conversion teaches us little, while sin is a great instructor. We learn much more from our pain than from our pleasure. We learn much more from letting go than from holding tight.

The task of the Church is to send you off on this journey, where you get to know the truth down in the gut and in the heart and even in the head, where you get to know it, as it were, through and through. It's not other people's experience or knowledge that matters but your own journey. None of us can take away the responsibility that God gives each person for himself or herself. Some say that "God has no grandchildren. God only has children." We can only transmit the experience of our ancestors.

We can trust ourselves to make this personal journey if at the same time we have the freedom to come together as brothers and sisters. If in this community you share your hearts with one another and you search yourselves honestly: "Am I crazy? Am I completely off base?" And if you give your brothers and sisters the right to say, "Yes, you're nuts." If you can ask them, "Do I love Jesus or am I in love with myself?" And if you give them the right to say, "Yes, you're more in love with yourself." This freedom is the mystery of the Church, where the Church becomes concrete.

In 1961 the pope asked us to send 10 percent of our personnel to Latin America. Nobody did it. Even people who claim that they obey the pope didn't do it. When I went to Latin America, I was told: "We're glad they didn't send any priests then. If the priests had come, things would have gone on the way they always had. This doesn't mean that we don't want to celebrate any Eucharists or that we don't want to have God's word preached. But we were forced to seek out our own way, and now we have a country like Brazil with between eighty and a hundred thousand base communities."

It seems to me that Jesus is renewing the Church, not from above but from below. The little communities need the large, universal history. Otherwise it can easily happen that they fall into cheap liberalism or narrow New Age thought, into things that have little social force because they once again concentrate on the privatized self. But conversely if we have only the large institution without the radical little group alongside it, then the institution turns into a cold, dead skeleton.

I come from the Franciscan tradition. Francis of Assisi didn't leave the Church as a rebel; very quietly he built a little chapel on the edge of the city. He learned to pray, he learned to surrender himself, he learned to let go. His life spoke prophetically, because in the final analysis we live our way into a new kind of thinking, while we in the West have always thought we could think our way into a new way of life. You have to run with your own feet to a place where you haven't been before — to a new place. You have to leave the world where you have everything under control, where everybody likes you, and head into a world where you are poor and powerless. And there you'll be converted despite yourself.

It often happens that the people we go to convert end up converting us, if we really have the freedom to take up their pain. I think this is what Jesus' healing is all about.

Jesus doesn't turn the people into Lutherans or Catholics; he touches their human pain. And people who "live among graves" suddenly find that through Jesus they have been freed from that pain.

Nothing that I'm suggesting can be accomplished by our thinking about it. For twenty years now I've been preaching all over the world — the sermons of priests and pastors convert no one. Just consider how many sermons you've already heard in your life. *Circumstances* convert people! You have to make your way to new circumstances, so that reality can really get through to you, because that's where Jesus has hidden himself: in the human condition and even in the humiliation of human flesh. Christ always comes into the world on an ass, Christ always comes into the world as a beggar. We would so much like to have him enclosed in the Church and in our theology. But God is always free.

Jesus defines freedom in an incredibly concrete manner. That's why Jesus says in Matthew 25 that we will be judged on the basis of only one thing. It has nothing philosophical about it, it has nothing at all to do with conservatism or liberalism, nor with whether you're right or wrong: either you do it or you don't. He says in effect: "There is only one thing you have to do. You must have the freedom to recognize me where you didn't expect me; otherwise you aren't free. And you will be judged on a single question: 'Could you recognize me in the least of your brothers and sisters?'"

Obviously those who did this were not in the least aware that they had met Christ. They didn't do it for Jesus; they simply did it. They didn't even talk about having a personal relationship with Jesus Christ. Please forgive me if this shocks you, but that's what it says in Matthew 25. Of course, I hope you do have a personal relationship with Jesus Christ; but there are people who have no such conscious relationship and nevertheless do Christ's truth. And many of us know the words but don't do the truth. And then later we discover Christ in a place where we never would have guessed he'd be. Until this transformation occurs, we can't call ourselves free.

I'd like to repeat: all this is nothing that we can do; it happens to us. The only thing we can do is get ourselves out of the way. Don't take yourselves too seriously. Be empty and open and ready; then Christ himself will be your teacher.

Nation-States Incapable of Salvation

I don't mean to imply that the capitalistic system has no value of any kind. But the Gospel frees us from making an idol of any system whatsoever. We must have the freedom to see the dark side of capitalism. If I were preaching in another economic system, I'd have to be just as critical. The Gospel always has to be preached in a social context — and the one we face in capitalism is different from the one in socialism.

When I read the New Testament, I don't get the impression that Jesus had a concrete plan for society that would go far beyond what I call *nonidolatry* or *letting go.* Jesus frees us from ourselves and from our illusions, so that genuine community becomes possible. But I can never expect any nation-state to understand anything like that. For far too long we have looked to the nation-state for our salvation; that's not its job. In his encyclical *Laborem Exercens,* when he speaks about capitalism and communism, the pope says that both are totalitarian systems, both are corrupt, and both exploit the Third World. Although this message has come from the pope, you don't often hear this viewpoint in the churches. We're used to the Church saying that socialism is false, but we wouldn't like the Church to uncover the dark side of capitalism. That was my intention here. In so doing I don't seek to shame us, but to contribute to our liberation. I'm a "capitalist" too. We have nothing to lose — unless we are addicted or at the top of the pile.

Emerging Perspectives on the Bible

I find it exciting that in our time the Gospel is finally being read through other eyes than just those of white, theologically educated men. And these other eyes come to altogether different insights — with the same Bible that we've been senselessly squabbling over for centuries.

For me there are four important new interpretations of the Bible: The first is to read it through the eyes of *women*. Women normally don't start right off by asking questions about power and control. Second, there's the reading of the Bible through the eyes of the *poor*. At the beginning of this century 70 percent of all Christians lived in North America and Europe. In the year 2000, 70 percent of all Christians lived in the Third World. And therein lies a great hope for the conversion of the Church. The third kind of exposition is through *community,* instead of the endless individualistic interpretations of the prosperous West. I came to know this above all in Africa, but also in other countries, where men and women still think as a group, as a tribe, as a people. For example, the first question asked by South Africans is, How can the whole tribe benefit? and not, How can I be saved? With the South Africans you can see that they live shoulder to shoulder in a sort of nonchoreographed unity. That's an altogether different way of living; communitarian people will read the Gospel in a completely different way. Not "How do I get saved?" as much as "Why are things this way?"

And the fourth new way of reading the Bible is with the eyes of the *mystics,* with the eyes of contemplatives. You find this everywhere throughout the world, but it seems to come most naturally to the people in Asia.

I think the primary gift that Europe and North America have to offer is that of biblical interpretation by women. And to some extent in my book *The Wild Man* I try to encourage men to look at their reality through the eyes of women too. Paradoxically this is just what makes them "wild men."

The Paradoxical Nature of Authentic Spirituality

I'm convinced that authentic spirituality is always paradoxical. I even think that any "common sense" that doesn't have a certain paradoxical character deserves to be distrusted. God takes me very seriously. But this frees me from the burden of having to do that chore myself. Perhaps it's a problem of semantics, but I can say that I take myself very seriously and at the same time not very seriously at all. And in the same moment both statements are entirely true.

A Holistic Approach to Service

If as a Catholic I may be allowed to say this, I believe the dark side of Protestantism consists in its being too much the prisoner of the left brain. The pulpit is enthroned as the center of the church's space, to move the *word* of God into the center. This is a good theological concern, but at the same time it has idolized and exalted the left side of the brain. It's given us the impression that we could unite people with words. That's absurd. We'll never all consent to the same words — that's why the Word became flesh. It was not enough for the Word to remain a word, it had to become flesh. And we Christians are still scandalized by the Incarnation.

In 1981 it was scientifically proved that there are two hemispheres in the brain with two quite different functions. The left brain analyzes reality. The left brain would have us believe that the knowledge and interpretation of all individual aspects are enough to understand the whole. This worldview sees things as either-or. The left brain can't deal with paradoxes; it can't process contradictions. The right half of the brain is exactly the opposite. The right brain recognizes reality through synthesis. It argues from its understanding of the whole back to the parts. And it comes to see reality through symbols and images. The right brain is concerned with things like symbols, song, or art. And of course both halves of the brain are "correct." But they're correct only when they allow the opposite side to be correct as well. That's why they're bound together by the corpus callosum. In the last thousand years we have increasingly neglected the right brain. That's the reason for the expansion of the "white male system." This system has an inner logic that serves to keep the system intact. It's logic is largely left-brain.

Jesus is much more holistic. He speaks and he acts. Then he goes on speaking and goes on acting. He touches, experiences, and lives reality in his body. He goes, for example, to the pagan, non-Jewish world, and lets a Syro-Phoenician woman tell him that he's wrong. He's ready to learn. He has a theology of the flesh.

I believe that the left and right halves of the brain are both wonderful gifts, but only when they work together to lead us to a more holistic view of reality. This is the case when we reach decisions, act, and commit ourselves to quite different positions. It can mean, for instance, that we take a step in solidarity toward the mentally handicapped, or that we involve ourselves with the pain and loneliness of the elderly or with AIDS patients. Somehow or other we have to get out of our own world and make room for the pain of other people. We won't manage this by logical reflection. And our ego will find a thousand excuses why we're not ready for it. But faith means giving away what we thought we didn't even have. That's what makes its faith.

My Left-Brain Ancestry

Paradoxically, I have to speak from the standpoint of the left hemisphere to help people free themselves from the left hemisphere. Moses held the serpent up in the air for those who had been bitten by serpents. But I grant that I too am a "left-brain" German: that's my gift and my cross. It was important to me, for example, that I've lived in a community with *women and children,* and that I now live in New Mexico with *Indians.* These two experiences have helped me to cross over a little more to the other side, to a more right-brain orientation.

The Dark Side of Catholicism

I wrote a book called *Why Be Catholic?*[15] The second chapter is "The Dark Side of Catholicism." Naturally some people bought the book just to read the second chapter. I believe that the dark side of Catholicism is its *triumphalism,* an exaggerated fascination with its own past, which was largely European. Although it calls itself "Catholic," i.e., all-embracing, to this day the Catholic Church has in fact remained largely a European Church. The dark side of Catholicism is its refusal to be *really* catholic, to be a truly universal Church.

The Catholic Church keeps falling into the trap of social prejudices. And because it has its foundation in Europe, the Catholic Church was very quickly imprisoned in the left half of the brain. In any case it does have an advantage over Protestantism: it has a *past* that was all-embracing and with which it can connect, for example, with the time when the wonderful medieval cathedrals were built, or when there were mystery plays in the church, when the Church knew something about music and art and produced contemplative mystics. But for the most part the Catholic Church has lost all that. But at least it's still present in our memory.

The Mystery of Powerlessness

I believe that one of the reasons why the Twelve Step programs of anonymous groups are so much in demand is that the first step involves a personal acknowledgement of powerlessness. The statement runs something like, "I admit to myself that I'm powerless and incapable of taking my own life in my hands." The teachers of these Twelve Step programs demand from the participants that they hand over their life not only to the group (e.g., of other alcoholics) but also to what is called in the programs a "higher power." Both through community and through faith the small self must surrender to the Great Self. Otherwise we get trapped inside of ourselves. I would be very disappointed if you interpreted my words as an invitation to individualism. Individualism would engender still more alcoholics. As an individual I must bear in my own private soul the whole burden of my goodness and my badness. But the teaching of the body of Christ liberates me precisely from this. Society is partially responsible both for my sin and for my virtue. We see this exemplified in our biblical story by the way the whole village participates in the imprisonment of an individual, while at the same time the village had the chance to participate in his emancipation.

Conversion through Circumstances

It's quite clear that in the final analysis it's the grace of Christ that liberates us. It's the experience of unconditional love that really sets us free. But first we have to be led to the circumstances that make it possible for this love to get through to us, so that we can sense and experience the *need* for this new life. I believe that it was precisely the circumstances that converted the man living among the graves. His experience was of being excluded. The pain of always being rejected was what finally made him capable of reaching out to Christ. And that's why Jesus often says that the tax-collectors and the drunkards are more open to the Reign of God than we theologians who have only theories in our heads. Surprisingly, and to many even shockingly, sinners have a certain head start in understanding spiritual things. Their small ego boundaries are taken from them through humiliation and failure, and they often literally must find God or disintegrate. We "nice" folks have avoided that necessary ego humiliation.

This statement by Jesus is an eternally valid judgment and a warning to us who deal with the Christian faith professionally: it's very dangerous to be a "professional Christian," to be possessed of theories of conversion and salvation. I believe that religion is the safest place to avoid God, because God wants to lead us to self-surrender, and all too often religion teaches us only self-control. And these are two completely different movements: genuine self-control is a *fruit* of the Spirit, but it's not the *cause* of the Spirit. Maybe Christ leads us *to* the circumstances and leads us *through* them back to God.

7

What Is This "Women's Stuff"?

෪෬

"Throughout the earth men spoke the same language, with the same vocabulary. But they said to one another, 'Come, let us build ourselves a town and a tower with its top reaching heaven.'" (Gen. 11:1, 4)

"In the world the powerful lord it over the others. This must not happen among you." (Luke 22:25–26)

We would probably not have to ask the question in my title if we had understood the lessons in these two Scripture passages.[16] The question is not just mine, but that of any male, who is also white, educated, middle-class, and even priestly. Each of these perspectives makes me less likely to be aware of "women stuff," much less see any problems or need to change anything. We white males have been holding all the cards, naming all the questions, and providing all the answers for the entire Christian era — except for those few golden years when God took poor flesh in Jesus. He took twelve Jewish men and tried to show them how they could be part of the solution instead of part of the problem. Unfortunately, it didn't work. Males continued to build towers and operate as lords over others, and women stuff just didn't fit in. That is the world and the Church that I was born into. It is preoccupied with domination and status-quo logic to this day and thus finds itself largely incapable of understanding, much less believing, most of the clear teaching of Jesus. Poverty, meekness or nonviolence, tears, justice-love, mercy, purity of heart, peacemaking and reconciliation, and bearing (persecution or what we might call "losing graciously") are his opening statements. But try to get elected in a Christian country or promoted to a Catholic bishopric today while following those teachings! Yet Jesus forthrightly called them the Eight Happinesses.

Apparently, Christian men of power have decided that happiness is optional. What is mandatory and necessary is that the world be divided into those who have the power and those who don't. It makes for good order, at least for those on top, and order is more important than happiness. Our word for this addictive view of reality is "patriarchy," which means the "rule of the fathers." It is the basis of all major relational systems in the Western world. In the patriarchal view (1) all relationships are eventually defined in terms of superiority and inferiority, and (2) the all-important need for order and control is assured by the exercise of dominative power. Now that does not sound so bad if the status quo happens to be working in your favor. But it has served to dehumanize and therefore despiritualize generations of races, nations, professions, women, sexual minorities, handicapped people, the weak and the elderly whom the powerful are able to disparage culturally and dismiss as being "of no account." Not only are the rich and powerful able to project their own darkness onto such groups, but the groups normally accept that darkness as their true value. The utter evil of such patriarchy is that both the oppressor and the oppressed are incapable of real spiritual growth. The powerful, by rejecting their shadow, are hopelessly inflated. The powerless, by receiving others' shadows, are endlessly deflated. Both lose.

Patriarchy is the nerve center of an entire worldview that idealizes winning over others, power and control (the outer face of fear), and the much abused philosophies of "might makes right" and "peace through strength." Without "success" (by his own definition) and control the patriarch does not know who he is. Many would honestly admit that such a life would not be worth living, which shows how deep the addiction has become. We must readily admit that many women are also patriarchs in this sense, or at least co-dependent members of the male system. They will often defend it even more feverishly than many males.

The language of patriarchy is always a noble or macho language of patriotism and freedom. Men (and their female echoes) are always speaking it, but the amazing thing is that anyone is still willing to believe it. But fortunately the poor, the oppressed and marginalized, and especially women are beginning to trust their natural and truly religious instincts. In some cases this leads them to mistrust and even disobey the cerebral and self-assured conclusions of the powers that be. You might call that arrogance and pride. You might also call it courage, or sometimes even faith. God will sort it out; I don't have to. Remember, I'm learning to give up my need for control and explanation!

We have to move toward the instinctual point since left-brain reason and logic have served us so poorly at this point in Western civilization. We find ourselves satisfied with two-thirds of our people either starving, unemployed, or homeless, while unthinkingly polluting and preparing to bomb the rest — and at the same time touting glorious phrases like freedom, free enterprise, "making the world safe for democracy," and our sacred "family values." Man's capacity to disguise his own darkness seems endless. Patriarchal logic is only logic in favor of the system and the status quo — which is proudly called "the real world." Believe me because I always hear it quoted to me after my sermons, usually from polite men in three-piece suits: "That was an interesting talk there, Father, but you know in the real world . . . " The fathers of the system hate nothing more than another father who refuses the rules of the game. That is precisely our role in proclaiming the new system that Jesus called the Reign of God. That's why he trained the twelve men to think and act in a new way. It's sort of a subversion-from-within tactic, but since we have not done very well at it, God is now sending the women to help us.

> **The language of patriarchy is always a noble or macho language of patriotism and freedom. Men (and their female echoes) are always speaking it, but the amazing thing is that anyone is still willing to believe it. But fortunately the poor, the oppressed and marginalized, and especially women are beginning to trust their natural and truly religious instincts.**

"Women stuff" is the hidden energy behind almost all the justice issues. The movement toward nonviolence and disarmament, the movements that deal with homelessness and refugee problems, with the raping of the earth and its resources, with sexual and physical abuse issues, with the idolatry of profit and the corporation, and with the rejection of the poor will not move beyond the present impasse until the underlying issues of power, prestige, and possessions are exposed for the lie that they are. Surprisingly, we are seeing that the power elites under any regime are just as opposed to change as are the wealthy and powerful under capitalism. Do you see what that tells us? Nations and governments are not the final enemy; powerful domination in every system wants to maintain its privilege. So also, maleness is not the problem, but male pretensions of power and winning. These towers of Babel have cost men their own souls for too long — along with the bodies, spirits, and dignity of much of the rest of the world.

Pyramids are always pyramids of sacrifice. Whether it is the hundreds of thousands of slaves creating monuments to Egyptian kings, the sacrificial victims offering their hearts to Aztec gods, or the underpaid maids and janitors in the tourist hotels of the world, someone always has to give his life or her life so that someone else can be "special." When that specialness is idealized and protected instead of avoided and made unnecessary, as Jesus taught, we see the destructive and dark side of power. Jesus struck at the nerve center of such power when he empowered honest human relationships instead of degrees of religious worthiness. Jesus built circles instead of pyramids. What they could not forgive him for, even on the cross, was that he announced the necessary destruction of the holy temple. "Not a stone will stand on a stone. Everything will be destroyed." (Mark 13:2) He knew that the temple, now divided into courts of worthiness, was not a place where God was first as much as a place that kept the central storehouse economy in control and the widow with her "mite" outside. Thus he revealingly called it "the treasury" (Mark 12:41) and committed the unforgivable sin of over-turning the tables of "those who were selling and buying there." (Luke 19:45) In attacking the temple, he attacked Judaism's final tower and democratized religion once and for all. But like the first priest, Aaron, we priests have been building golden calves and golden temples ever since. With priests and ministers, the assumption is that if it is good for religion, it is good for God. "False!" said Jesus.

In the tower of Babel incident referred to at the begin-ning of this chapter, God had to scatter and confuse the one language of the men who had built the pretentious tower "to make a name for" themselves. (Gen. 11:4) Here we have the anomaly of a God who separates and divides people when they have structured themselves wrongly. In an early style of perestroika, God reverses this process at Pentecost when tongues of fire unite the different lan-guages into one universal language of the Spirit: "each hearing in their own language about the wonderful works of God." (Acts 2:11) Circles of communication, networks of nations, true brotherhood and sisterhood are finally pos-sible in this new people who are born of God's Spirit. And it is no accident that God the Spirit is presented in a feminine and maternal image from which we are "born." (John 3:5–8) Immediately after the giving of the Pente-cost Spirit we have the further birth of real and honest community: "The faithful all lived together and owned everything in common; they sold their goods and posses-sions and shared out of the proceeds according to each one's need." (Acts 2:44–45) We can only imagine fondly since it has rarely happened again. Francis of Assisi tried. The vow of poverty was an attempt. But the patriarchal need for domination and possession preferred towers and basilicas to human community, degrees of worthiness instead of honest human relationships. Dare I list the line-up? Pope, curia, cardinals, metropolitans, archbishops, bishops, vicar generals, monsignors, priests, deacons, subdeacons (rejected as unnecessary!), exorcists, acolytes, lectors, and porters constitute the *cleros,* or "separated ones." If there is any worthiness left, it is graciously dispensed to the *laos,* the 99 percent of the membership who are told exactly how they can be worthy. Forgive my sarcasm, but it is intentional and long overdue. God's reputation is at stake.

The feminine insight is a rediscovery of Jesus' spirit, a reemergence of a well-suppressed truth, an eventual political upheaval, a certain reform of our hearing of the Gospel and someday perhaps the very structures of the churches — and all proceeding from a "knowing" in the mother's womb, the exact place from which we received Christ for the first time.

It was no accident that we Catholics had a psychological need to exalt Mary to the role of a goddess. I am not sure if it was an inherent need to balance ourselves, a disguise for the patriarchy underneath, a love affair with the denied woman within, or just a work of the Spirit, but it is an overwhelming example of instinct winning out over logic and theology. So much so, in fact, that the only two infallible statements of this Roman patriarchal Church are ironically the Assumption of the physical body of Mary into heaven and her privileged choice and protection by God called the "Immaculate Conception." Furthermore, we even celebrate her "Coronation as Queen of heaven and earth." I'm really all for it, but none of these are found in Scripture or public revelation. Amazing how this male Church was always feminist — and unwittingly ready to bend all the rules to say so! That healthy instinct has now come to our service and we call it "women stuff." Sorry, boys, we Catholics have always been there. Proud and orthodox in public, but Mama's boys whenever we could find an excuse for it. It's not new or liberal or dangerous; it's very old, quite conservative, and as traditional as Mary and the Eight Beatitudes.

The feminist insight explains the vast majority of Jesus' teachings, a male acting very differently in an almost totally patriarchal Jewish society. Like Mary, the Church also has "treasured these things in her heart." (Luke 2:19) Only in time are they ready to come forth, like Jesus from her womb. Jesus would never have broken through as the fresh Word of the Father if he had, for example, acted nonviolently in a feminine body. It would not have been Divine Revelation because we expect and demand that *women* be patient, nurturing, forgiving, healing, self-effacing, and self-sacrificing. Women are expected to be nonviolent in a violent male society (look at our one-sided attitude toward rape, adultery, physical abuse, and, in many cultures, divorce), but we are still not prepared for males or institutions or nations to act nonviolently. That is why God *had* to become incarnate for us in the body of a man. Unfortunately, we kept the name and image of Jesus to exalt male leadership, but basically rejected most of Jesus' teachings as impractical and unreasonable in the pyramidal "real world" of Church and state. As indeed they are! We conveniently fit Jesus back into our more practical way of being a religious institution — and lost most of his unique and revolutionary strategy for dealing with human evil. Now we find ourselves helpless and without the tools to deal with war, greed, and the endless whimsy of the individual ego.

No one was wicked or intentional in all of this, nor is it all wrong and lost, but it does show the depth and disguise of evil. Power is surely not intrinsically wrong, but it is very dangerous and, in my opinion, only spiritually mature people can handle it. Power, another word for the Spirit in Scripture, is most effective when it is clearly recognized as such and clearly shared as a common but diverse gift. At Pentecost the Spirit came down on "all," (Acts 2:1) giving them the power to recognize and affirm life within themselves and in one another. That is the richest meaning of authority. It is the power to author life in others. That power is not exclusively or even primarily held by men. It seems to me that should be self-evident. At the present moment of history, unbalanced male consciousness has given us both totalitarian communism and greedy capitalism, neither of them seeking the common good of humanity. Both are pyramids of sacrifice, afraid of circles of truth and justice.

I see nothing in the New Testament that tells me Jesus intended or desired his new community to be modeled on the power structures of the Roman Empire. Further, I see nothing in the life narrative of Peter the fisherman that tells me he can be expected to do anything but doubt, bungle, deny, and run. But he also professes love and stands as a full prophetic image of the de facto life of the hierarchy and the Church. Jesus' love of Peter tells me that he is willing to work with just such human brokenness — just as he is willing to work with all the rest of the world that is unsuitable, out of order, unorthodox, and even sinful. That, unfortunately, is what patriarchy is unwilling and unable to do. It demands an infallible pope and a "worthy" people. The love of power does not have the capacity to nurture anything that it cannot explain or control. The exclusive rule of the fathers not only makes community and justice impossible but also holds Christ's salvation at the level of salvation theories and techniques that educated clerics can be "right" about. The starving millions deserve a better God than that. They deserve the Father that Jesus knew.

The feminist insight explains the vast majority of Jesus' teachings, a male acting very differently in an almost totally patriarchal Jewish society.

The Father that Jesus knew looks amazingly like what most cultures would call "Mother." In Luke 15, the story of the prodigal son, Jesus makes his most complete presentation of the character of this Father, whom he called God. The father is in every way the total opposite of the male patriarch and even rejects his older son's appeal from a world of worthiness and merit. He not only allows the younger son to make choices against him, but even empowers him to do so by giving him the money! After his bad mistakes, the father still refuses his right to restore order or impose a penance even though the prodigal son offers to serve as a hired servant. Both his leaving and his returning are treated as necessary but painful acts of adult freedom. In every way he can, the father makes mutuality and vulnerability possible. As Sr. Sandra Schneiders says, this new kind of father "refuses to own us, demand our submission, or punish our rebellion. Father God is one who respects our freedom, mourns our alienation, waits patiently for our return, and accepts our love as pure gift.... God tries to educate the older brother, and through him all disciples who prefer the security of law to the adventure of grace." In an absolutely reeling conclusion, she says, "The power God refuses to assume over us is surely not given by God to any human being." Not even to the Church that must always live in the image of the heavenly Father.

All this "woman stuff" is not only important, it is the other half of conversion, the other half of salvation, the other half of wholeness that completes God's work of art. I believe this mystery is imaged in the Woman of the twelfth chapter of the Apocalypse: "pregnant, and in labor, crying aloud in the pangs of childbirth ... and finally escaping into the desert until her time."

Could this be the time? I think it must be. The world is tired of Pentagons and pyramids, empires and corporations that only abort God's child. The West is alive with liberation movements at every level of consciousness, with race, gender, and economic issues (prestige, power, and possessions!) at the forefront. Even the Church is finding the humility to recognize its fear of the subjective and the personal and its unlawful marriage to the systems of power and control. The woman is coming out of her desert escape, with no possibility of return. Too many of us have seen her gift. The Holy Child Wisdom is among us and the vision is compelling. We *can* live and think differently.

Yes, this woman stuff is very important, more than this white male priest ever imagined or desired! My God was too small and too male; now I don't know how to fight with a woman. What I, what we, need to learn is to love Her, to recognize and affirm Her gifts, to understand that She is intrinsic to divine and human wholeness.

Authentic faith has something to do with fighting God, and I'm not sure I know how best to engage with a God who is also feminine. I know the rules of the game for struggling with a man, but I have less understanding of how you struggle with a woman. That's also surely connected to the fact that I'm not married.

The Need for a Maternal Face of God

I believe in the Trinity. But still I agree with Christa Mulack that we have to find the maternal face of God. I believe it's both helpful and natural to look on the Spirit/Spiritess as feminine. We can also say that the power of the relationship that occurs between the Father and the Son is something feminine in the sense that it is intimate, mutually vulnerable, an unhindered dialogue. These qualities can apply to men also, but most cultures associate them with women and the feminine. I believe that in the Christian tradition there have always been people who by means of prayer have pressed through to find the female face of God. This is certainly one of the possibilities for correctly integrating into our faith the medieval veneration of Mary, or even later forms of piety like the veneration of the Sacred

Heart. Somehow we have always sensed that our image of God is too masculine. That's why we've tried in different ways to venerate this female face of God as well. In Genesis it says point blank: we are made in the image of God, masculine and feminine. From this statement alone it should be obvious that God is not a man, but that men and women reflect the image of God. I don't believe, however, that this means we have to give up the doctrine of the Trinity.

America's Need to Encounter Its Shadow

Jesus often asked sadly, "When the Son of man comes, will he find faith on earth?" It was obvious to Jesus that he would always represent a minority position. He saw clearly that his community would always remain a little flock. And nevertheless one has to say that all over the world you can sense a growing awareness of the dignity of the individual. There is a growing distrust of power, dictatorships, and mechanisms of oppression. But our country is built on a mythology of power, and it'll be very hard to deprive the system of its power. America has to acknowledge its shadow. I believe the Vietnam War was the encounter with our shadow, but we forgot about it too quickly.

Mary and the "Madonna Complex"

I believe it's important that we let Mary be a *person*. As Catholics we have drifted too far in the opposite direction. An image of Mary as one of us helps us to identify with her and to duplicate her attitude. In this way she'll much more readily become a graphic image for the Church and for salvation. You can put someone on a pedestal and thereby prevent any authentic relation with that person. When we do this with women it's called in psychology the "Madonna complex." We put Mary on such a lofty pedestal that she is unreachable, nonimitable, and cannot serve her elevating function for humanity. In Latin America they have no difficulty discovering in the Magnificat that Mary is a woman who fights with them for liberation down at the grassroots level. She does this, of course, in the persona of a poor woman from Nazareth — and not as the larger-than-life Mother of God. That's why I suggest we love Mary as a *woman* who was chosen by God.

8

The Social and Political Vocation of Christians

❧

PAUL TELLS US that the word of God is a perfect mirror of freedom.[17] I believe the first task of God's word is to confront us with ourselves, with our truth. And this confrontation will lead, we hope, to changing our lives, to building our lives on the great truth that Jesus calls the "Reign of God." It seems to me that only after we've changed our lives does the Gospel promise comfort. In my opinion the great danger facing prosperous Christians is that we have exactly reversed this process. We let ourselves be comforted first, before letting the perfect mirror of freedom confront us with ourselves. And that's why our religion remains so schizophrenic.

Among Christians there are pray-ers and activists. The activists don't understand anything about prayer, and the prayers of the pious seldom lead to involvement. The spread of the Gospel suffers, basically because it is not "good news" for anybody. Neither of the two has the whole Christ or real credibility. Our Bible texts will explain how different the call these people receive must be. In the tenth chapter of Mark two different "callings" follow in rapid succession, first the calling of the rich young man and then of the blind man Bartimaeus. First I will discuss the section on Jesus and the rich young man. (Mark 10:17–27)

"As he was setting out on his journey, a man ran up and knelt before him, and asked him, 'Good Teacher, what must I do to inherit eternal life?' " Observe that the rich young man is very polite and very respectful toward Jesus. But we notice right away that Jesus doesn't take the bait of this flattery. He knows the danger of a language that's too nice, while really seeking to keep the other at arm's length. (We've found that the word "nice" does not occur once in the New Testament. But bourgeois Christianity continually revolves around being "nice.") "And Jesus said to him: 'Why do you call me good? No one is good but God alone.' " Jesus immediately points beyond himself. Isn't that interesting? If *we* said that Jesus wasn't good, we'd be treated as heretics. Jesus wanted people to come to grips with reality, not with ideals and images. Images and ideals allow us to remain in love with ourselves, but Jesus preferred us to be in love with truth.

That's why his answer comes out sounding brusque and not very understanding. He simply lists the Commandments ("Do not kill, Do not commit adultery, Do not steal, Do not bear false witness") in the proper order of the Commandments as we know them. But before he mentions the Fourth Commandment ("Honor your father and mother") he makes a little insertion: "Do not defraud." Where does that come from? It's not one of the Ten Commandments; it's evidently what he's reproaching the young man for. The young man, belonging to the large landowners, naturally wants to defend himself right away and prove that despite his wealth he is, religiously speaking, justified: "Teacher, all these I have observed from my youth." He has completely missed the point of Jesus' adding the line, "Do not defraud."

Jesus straightway looks at him and loves him. He knows that justice isn't possible until we've experienced love. He knows that this man's sin is at bottom not a personal thing, but a kind of objective dilemma that he's trapped in. That's why he tries to tell him how he can get out of the lie he's caught in, how he can again ground his life on the truth instead of on lies.

"Jesus said, 'You lack one thing; go, sell what you have, and give to the poor.' " That's what you have to do; otherwise you won't be free. Because your money builds on a lie, and you have to base your life on the truth. "And you will have treasure in heaven." Only when you face this challenge can you "come, follow me." Again, the rich young man isn't personally bad; he's simply part of the system in which he's stuck. And Jesus calls him to distance himself from it. This is the only example in the Gospel of Mark of a person called by Jesus who becomes a nonfollower, a nondisciple. "At that saying his countenance fell, and he went away sorrowful, for he had great possessions." We notice that every time Jesus challenges those who have power and wealth he never calls them personally evil or malevolent. Instead he points to the fact that they're blind, that they can't see. He tells them that they have to leave this system, because otherwise they'll never learn to see.

Thus women, the poor, and the base communities are raising altogether different questions, and altogether different answers will come to light. We can no longer so easily thrust aside, as we used to, the unequivocal message of the sort of passage we have just now read.

For far too long we've preached the Gospel only in an individualistic fashion. We thought we could have a personal relationship with Jesus without calling into question the systems and institutions we participate in and to which we belong. In my first few years of work with young people in Cincinnati, I preached the Gospel and the young people fell in love with Christ. They believed that they were converted, that they were "saved." When they tried to integrate their lives inside of the overpowering American culture, it was usually the culture that won. Genuine evangelization must be good news for the individual and *at the same time* for society, for the nation, for the institution. The great blind spot of European and American Christianity is that we can't see that the Gospel isn't aimed just at the individual, but also at society. We have read it so long as a "private salvation theory" that we do not realize the entire Bible is first of all a "salvation of history" and a liberation of "a people" and humanity for God. Yes, it starts with individuals "getting it," but they will go deep only if they can be contained and carried by a community, a culture, and a "church." In my experience, individuals start groups and movements, but then those groups either purify or destroy that very individual. It is the group or the movement that has the final say and the strongest voice. I see this again and again and have even seen it in my experience in both Cincinnati and Albuquerque. Both of the groups that I supposedly "founded" purified me by almost destroying me, but without them my message was impotent.

Perhaps the poor see themselves in the second part of chapter 10 of Mark's Gospel, namely, with the calling of the poor blind man, Bartimaeus. We see a paradox here: Bartimaeus is the blind man who isn't blind—in contrast to the rich man, who's really poor. Between these two stories Mark presents a great warning from Jesus against the real enemies of the Reign of God. These are the three great obsessions: power, prestige, and possessions. In the Sermon on the Mount it's quite clear that these are the three great barriers we have to overcome to understand Jesus and the Reign of God. But in Christianity we have always been concerned with ecclesiological questions, sacramental questions, sacerdotal questions, and, needless to say, sexual questions — questions that Jesus practically never bothered with.

It seems to me as if a kind of shadow screen gets slipped between us and Jesus here, so that we don't have to see the real questions. This is called a diversionary tactic. We probably choose it unconsciously and in all innocence because our ego finds enormously tricky ways to avoid self-surrender. Our ego finds incredibly imaginative ways to avoid letting go — even as we claim to believe in the absolute authority of the Bible. Let's all be honest and admit that our various denominations have one and all been only selectively obedient and have picked out only certain Bible verses that backed up our theological biases.

But every time Jesus deals with the real problems of this world, namely, with power and control, and with economic questions that would demand real change from us (not just changes in the head, but in our whole life), all the churches — without exception — have shoved those teachings aside and ignored them. None of us is ready for the great Christ, for the whole Christ; none of us is ready for the story that Christ offers us — except for poor blind people like Bartimaeus.

And they came to Jericho; and as he was leaving Jericho with his disciples and a great multitude, Bartimaeus, a blind beggar, the son of Timaeus, was sitting by the roadside. And when he heard that it was Jesus of Nazareth, he began to cry out and say, "Jesus, Son of David, have mercy on me!" And many rebuked him, telling him to be silent; but he cried out all the more, "Jesus, Son of David, have mercy one me!" (Mark 10:46–48)

This poor man isn't polite like the rich man. He shouts, he interrupts what's going on; and we see immediately how the disciples get irritated because he's not abiding by the appropriate rules of etiquette. And we see how his words differ from the words of the rich young man: the rich young man asks: How can *I* get eternal life? He's concerned with himself; it *is* a kind of enlightened egoism, but it's still egoism. And a large part of Christianity has so far refused to admit how egotistical it actually is. We've claimed we love Christ, but in reality this has been just a protective façade that hides our understandable self-interest. In Bartimaeus we see someone who's not asking anything at all for himself; he simply cries out twice for mercy. He knows that he's empty. He knows that he has nothing of what perhaps he should or must have.

This time it's Jesus who goes to him — the opposite of what happened in the first story. "And Jesus stopped and said, 'Call him.' And they called the blind man, saying to him, 'Take heart; rise; he is calling you.' " Even the disciples are surprised that Jesus is obviously interested in this completely useless person. The gestures of this blind man are the exact reverse of the rich young man's gestures: "And throwing off his mantle, he sprang up and came to Jesus." Here we see a man who's not covering himself, but giving himself away. He springs up full enthusiasm, and Jesus asks him: "What do you want me to do for you?"

This time Jesus takes the initiative: he knows that he really can give this man something — the rich young man wasn't open to it. With this man there's an openness, a readiness, an emptiness. He's full of desire, full of longing. "And the blind man said, 'Master, let me receive my sight.' "

> **Genuine evangelization must be good news for the individual and *at the same time* for society, for the nation, for the institution. The great blind spot of European and American Christianity is that we can't see that the Gospel isn't aimed just at the individual, but also at society.**

We have on the one hand the rich man, who thinks he can see but who in reality can see nothing, and, as a counter-image, the blind man, who can't see and yet in reality does see. "And Jesus said to him, 'Go your way; your faith has made you well.' " He doesn't say, your orthodoxy, your correct doctrine has made you well; he doesn't say, your obedience to the Commandments has made you well. The rich young man is anxious to prove to Jesus that he has kept all the Commandments. We have no proof that this blind man ever did anything "right" in his life, but Jesus says: " 'Go your way; your faith has made you well.' And immediately he received his sight and followed him on *the way.*" And we know what this "way" means if we read the next verse, because the first verse of chapter 11 says: "They drew near to Jerusalem." This is no gentle Gospel. We're evidently talking about the way of the cross, about a way of imitation and discipleship that calls upon us to surrender and let go.

But we must honestly confess that the Gospel has in many ways been lured into a trap by our society and culture. The Gospel is for the most part held by cultures of affluence. Ours is a society where we not only need more and more things, but where we keep demanding more and where we think we have a right to keep getting more. Our whole feeling of self-worth depends on our getting more, on our doing more, on our always climbing higher and higher. And that's why the story of the rich young man is intended for us.

If we read through the Gospels, we notice that there is a back-and-forth to Jesus' teachings: one time he preaches the Gospel to the oppressors and another time to the oppressed. Unfortunately it's the "victors" who almost every time reject and refuse him. And it's the victims of this world who almost always understand him. It almost looks as if we have to be marginalized to become at all capable of hearing the Gospel. On the margin the social and political implications of the Gospel become quite obvious and clear. There we learn that we can't use Jesus to defend and maintain our position of power and wealth or to keep up for our own sake a positive self-image as polite and decent people.

It could be that Jesus will lead us to a place where we ourselves don't even know whether we're holy, where all we know is that we have work to do, where we have to obey the word that we've heard in our heart. In this place we often don't even get the satisfaction of being in the right; and there's no security that everyone will agree with us. Perhaps that's why Jesus says, "I chose you out of the world, and therefore the world hates you." (John 15:19) This Gospel doesn't bless the existing system; it leads us to the edges where freedom might be found. It does so in such a way that we can return to the world, without being addictively dependent on it any more. We are able to return to the suffering and joys of this world, without letting ourselves be seduced by its false promises on either side.

I think a large part of Jesus' teaching is a critique of "mammon sickness." Jesus describes that disease as follows: those afflicted by it are continually driven by unrest, cares, and anxiety, because the present isn't enough for them. But for those grounded in Christ the present contains great abundance, even though we don't yet live in the full Reign of God. This is precisely the peace that the world can't give, and the peace the world can't take away from us. It's the only real gift we can bring into the existing system: the health (*salus*) of a centered life.

No political system, no explanation of the world can be anything other than a mixture of what is and is not the Reign of God. Of course, it's our responsibility to carry as much as possible of the Reign of God into this world, but no social or political system will ever equate to the Reign of God. Yet if we live in the fullness of the Here and Now — and this is the gift of the crucified and simultaneously risen Christ — then we no longer run around anxiously to get a definitive explanation of the world; we can live with *what is.*

Several years ago I was with Jim Wallis in Germany. We had worked a great deal with the peace movement at the time, and we had preached in many parts of the country as we had in the U.S. We took part in protests, we prayed, and we studied the issues of war and peace. After we had done all that, suddenly this fellow Gorbachev appeared, and the old rigid fronts started to move. Even if it seemed that the "New Jerusalem" was on the point of descending from heaven, we couldn't claim that our work had produced its arrival. Nevertheless, I believe our work was somehow important too. God never comes uninvited, it seems to me, and our little projects are an invitation and welcome to the final action of God. Because why should God give us something that we don't even want? Why should God give us something for which we're not ready to work and do our utmost? Why should God give us something that we at most pray for, but don't strive for? God doesn't believe just in our prayers. That's why we do our work, launch protests, and at the same time wait every moment for the "New Jerusalem" to descend from the heavens. I believe this is the great mystery of co-creation to which God has invited us. Mammon disease makes us completely deaf and blind to this full reality.

Many years ago I was invited to dinner by a family in Cincinnati (it's always nice to invite the pastor). This nice Italian family had three charming children. The youngest was named Christopher; he had big brown eyes, and he had just learned to run. After dinner he ran through the living room and fell down the stairs. But afterward we didn't hear a sound or any crying, so we were very worried because we didn't know whether he had injured himself. So we ran to the stairway, and there Christopher lay at the foot of the stairs. And his big brown eyes looked up inquiringly at his father, as if to say, "Did I hurt myself?" His father ran down to him, took him in his arms, and the instant his father's arms enfolded him, the boy began to scream and cry. I wondered why this little boy needed seven seconds before he felt pain, but at the same moment the answer occurred to me (and I knew at once that this would be a terrific example for a sermon): the little boy couldn't feel and admit the pain until he was sufficiently sure that love was there.

It seems to me that a Christian is a person who has the freedom to feel the pain that's part of being human. This means a person who has the freedom to enter into solidarity with the suffering of the world, precisely because this person is sure of God's love. Without that love we're deaf and our feelings go numb. And we can't spend our whole lives desperately trying to experience this love again; we have to go beyond basic evangelization to the purifying, maturing, and unitive stages of spirituality. Because we have not done this, Christianity has become a comic caricature in many parts of the world, a straw person that people quickly blow over without ever experiencing the wonderful "New Man" that Paul so rightly speaks of. (Eph. 2:15) In general, Protestants are much better at what I call "stage one evangelization," leading people to an initial experience of God and Christ, but it does not go very deep or become very integrated. Catholics and Orthodox are much better at the later stages, but it does little good because a high percentage of the laity have never had any real experience of Christ. As the author of Hebrews would say, we need both "milk and solid food." (5:11–14) We also need one another.

The problem with so many churches in our country is that every worship service tries to produce step one of Christian existence. And that's why we don't get many mature, grown-up Christians, but often very childish Christians who are concerned with their own feelings and nothing else. The final effect of mammon disease is that we've lived with a split consciousness, incapable of really integrating faith with the tragic mystery of things.

The split is so strong in our cultures that people who live entirely in the world of business, finance, insurance, or merchandising find the language of spirituality almost incomprehensible and totally uninteresting. If money doesn't quite explicitly and in all its consequences come under God's Reign, it won't remain a neutral force very long; it will seize dominion for itself. When we speak of God's sovereignty, we too often mean a nominal and honorary sovereignty, not a real one that has consequences, that changes our lifestyle in this world.

In America we say, "Money talks." I'm afraid money is the *only* thing doing the talking! Although we claim that Jesus is the Lord, it's obvious that in reality power, prestige, and possessions are the lords. Of course this holds us back from the freedom of the true children of God. I don't believe that there's a concrete goal, in the sense of one particular kind of job or task that is inherently better than another. In other words, I believe that a compassionate bartender or jailer would bring much more of God into the world than a cynical priest or minister. Jesus seems to teach a style and a process inside of the supposedly secular world much more than trying to pull us out of it into some rarefied sanctity.

He calls us to a way of life that is forgiving, trusting, and does not hold on, but lets go. It is a new way of seeing, so that human community is possible. I don't presume to be so clever as to know what the ideal community should look like. My task is to live the Reign of God here and now — not just privately for myself, but in an interconnected way, that is, a way that influences my economy, my finances, and my political position, that influences how I use the goods of this earth. This is the way of Bartimaeus. It's the way of the blind man who in reality isn't blind at all. I believe that the Gospel invites us all to enter upon this way.

The Proper Place of Mammon

As I have said, we have to find the place of real freedom from which we can return into the world. Jesus was not against possessions on principle; He was against idol worship. As soon as we *really* abjure this world's money, we have the freedom to use that money and do some good with it. But we have to keep on examining ourselves so that we don't deceive ourselves. It's easy enough to repeat the saying, "I'm in the world, but not of it," but as we all know, it is much harder to really achieve that delicate balance.

We have to discover very concretely and specifically how badly, for example, we identify with money. Only when our money is taken away do we learn how much we're possessed by our possessions. Don't think this awareness can take place in your head. The father of my order, Francis of Assisi, was fully convinced that poverty has to take in a concrete dimension. This is an altogether practical matter, when we consider how many billion people live on this little planet. We have to find real and realistic ways to be brothers and sisters to these people. The goods of this world have to be used, of course, but in a way that's honest and in which sharing plays a much larger role.

Escaping the System

There was a woman named Dorothy Day, the founder of the Catholic Worker. Because of her, all over America today there are houses for the homeless and people in need of shelter. This woman lived a life of poverty. She said, "I'd like to live my life so close to the bottom that when the system collapses I don't have far to fall."

Of course, the more we're tied up in the system, the fewer questions we can ask. I wonder, for example, why Jesus said we shouldn't take oaths? One interpretation is that every oath is a promise we make to a system. We must call into question the "oaths" we've made to institutions and armies. Our only commitment must be to the Body of Christ and to humanity. No individual can carry the cross alone. Only when groups of radical young people get together can they create a kind of counter-system that sees to it that they're less dependent on the old system. I think this is one of the reasons many of us have spent time building communities. It was a sad experience for me that most of the well-known lay communities, intentional communities, and "covenant communities" that emerged in the 1970s disintegrated over time. We cannot deny, however, that these communities were a wonderful school for thousands of people. In the last analysis they were a first-rate, hands-on school for life and ministry more than enduring communities as such. That is good. They created a network of "ties that bind," a network of community-minded people, of men and women who know how to connect with others, how to share, how to let go. I say this so that you yourselves may contribute to creating such networks. Without them there's no practicable method for standing outside the status quo.

Building a Better Political Structure

I wouldn't want you to take what I've said as anti-structural. I'm simply objecting to the idolization of any given structure as the perfect one. The patriarchal image of God has seduced us into building up and idealizing pyramidal structures. If I understand Jesus correctly, he seems to talk more about circles than about pyramids. His first description of the Church is "two or three who are gathered in my name." But when unredeemed men place themselves at the top, they create pyramids. And pyramids are always built on the sacrifices of others. To build the Egyptian pyramids hundreds of thousands of slaves had to give their lives; the Mayan temples were built so that human sacrifices could be offered on top of them.

When more feminine insights gain greater influence, better structures too will slowly develop; they'll be shaped less like pyramids and more like circles. I'm concerned about creating a world where it's possible to live as brothers and sisters. We pastors quarrel over what the true priest should look like, about who has the true theology, who gets to heaven and who doesn't. These are the chimeras of academically educated males. We need circles where we can be vulnerable and honest, where the prevailing atmosphere is one of healing and sharing of wisdom.

The Danger of Wealth

I also don't mean to imply that we shouldn't deal with economic issues. But the contemplative attitude takes the liberty of not knowing the solution to such things. Haven't we as Christians always had the feeling that we had to have the answer to everything? Why have we made faith into a kind of security blanket? We've taken what for Jesus was a journey into the unknown and turned in into a life insurance policy. I'd be glad to find a clear economic plan in the Gospel; but the only thing Jesus gave us unequivocal enlightenment about was the great danger of wealth. He said quite clearly that we're not supposed to get rich. We live differently in the poverty and ignorance of faith — which consists in our having no plan. Faith has a much higher price than I ever would have expected; the willingness to walk in darkness makes other people see you as naive.

The Pros and Cons
of the Charismatic Movement

My community, "New Jerusalem," was for a time one of the most exciting and lively charismatic communities in the country. And around the beginning of the 1970s I had the reputation of being the great charismatic pastor of young people. But ultimately I too realized that the charismatic

movement had its shadow side. First, it's much too dependent on feelings. You don't mature in the faith if you need
too many emotional experiences — that's quite obvious. In
my opinion the charismatic movement has an exaggerated
resurrection theology and a fear of the cross. That's why
you find there only half the paschal mystery. (In *Discovering
the Enneagram* I call this the energy of the SEVEN, but that's
only one of the possible ways of describing the matter.)

On the other hand, the charismatic movement is a
wonderful point of departure. Some of the most effective
social activists in our country spent two or three years during the 1970s in prayer groups. They themselves admit
that the charismatic experience taught them the immedi-
acy and the warmth of the love of God. They learned there
to thirst after holiness. But these same people also say that
after two or three years they stopped growing, that nothing
new unfolded. It's a wonderful, maybe even *necessary,* first
step of faith, and I mean that quite seriously, but the next
steps simply don't happen there. We must be led beyond
the world of feelings into the world of real faith, where we
don't continually have to reactivate first emotions. Mature
faith knows its ground and yet is also able to include and
integrate.

The best point of departure is conservative, because first
you need a clear feeling for your own boundaries. First, you
have to learn: what does it mean to be in Christ, or not to
be in Christ? You see this psychologically in every person
who grows in his or her faith: the more you become sure of
your own center, the more you can also open your boundaries. Otherwise you'll spend your whole life defending
those boundaries. This is like a litmus test for recognizing

immature Christianity. Nevertheless we have to be patient and allow ourselves to take certain steps toward growth. A mature Christian is capable of going beyond all previous boundaries and suddenly discovering Christ where he or she would never have suspected.

I think this is the clear meaning of the story in chapter 25 of Matthew: the people were suddenly able to discover Christ in the least of their brothers and sisters, and not just in other charismatics, not just with other evangelicals. Otherwise, all you have is a collective self-love. Then the group is, so to speak, just an extension of my own ego. This is evident in the need to use the same Christian jargon as I do, so that we can be together. But this isn't the freedom of the children of God. Such people will never unite or reconcile anything, because their life at bottom keeps getting smaller and smaller. Real Christians are able to discover and love Christ in the not-me, in the totally other — but this always means taking a step beyond previous boundaries. I don't believe that the charismatic movement has really given its members the capacity to do that, in any case not in our country. Nevertheless I repeat: it helps a great deal in the first stage of faith. Our overintellectual interpretation of the Gospel has needed the charismatic movement to get out its cerebral box.

The Way of Real Change

I chose the story of the rich young man to demonstrate the change we seek has to be very concrete, very immediate, and very practical. Otherwise it's just an intellectual thing. Jesus asks the rich young man to move from here to there —

and he meant economically. For most of us this means turning to people who are different from us. This is the only thing that can liberate us from our egocentric attitude. Maybe it means that as younger men and women we go to the elderly, or maybe as healthy persons we go to the physically and mentally handicapped, or if we're homophobic we work in an AIDS hospital. But we all have to set out into a world in which we're not number 1, where the others whom we meet are not just an expanded version of ourselves.

I believe that circumstances change us, not sermons. We're changed when we move on to a new place and when we expose ourselves to the truth of a different standpoint, one that's not our own. What else is *metanoia,* or conversion, supposed to mean in the New Testament? It means to go to a different place; and this practical step will see to it that our growth as Christians is something real, something earthbound. Otherwise there is always the danger that our so-called love of Christ will be just a disguised love of self.

Religion is a very dangerous business. I believe it's the surest way to avoid God. The scribes and the Pharisees in the Bible illustrate this well enough. If spiritual conversion doesn't lead us to letting go of and surrendering our lives and being able to go beyond ourselves, I believe it remains just an illusion; not real love of God but love of self. I know this from my own experience.

Socialism, Capitalism — or Neither?

The systems of socialism and capitalism both strike me as showing the incapacity of Christians to integrate what belongs together. If we had lived and taught a holistic Gospel of justice and peace, socialism would not have had to co-erce people into sharing. If we had taken seriously Jesus' lifestyle of poverty and simplicity, the Western capitalist countries, which are the very ones that call themselves Christian, would have never been able to move to this level of greed, unfettered ambition, and conspicuous con-sumerism. It's very easy for us in the capitalistic West to lean back and say: "Look, everything they were doing over there was wrong." But socialism basically grew out of the failure, and followed the pattern, of Western Christianity.

I believe that's why we have to find a third way in between these two systems: some kind of free communi-tarianism that seeks and protects the common good. John Paul II, whom the world considers a total enemy of social-ism, actually recommends a form of "modified socialism" in the majority of his social encyclicals. He rightly points out that "rigid capitalism" is just as evil for the world as is "totalitarian communism." This is seldom talked about in polite American circles of Catholics.

When I took the vow of poverty and promised to share all material goods with other Franciscans, why did people say, "How holy and wonderful that is!" while when people under a socialist system do it, it's suddenly called evil? Of course, the difference was that we did it voluntarily, and the others are forced to do it. The gift of our capitalist sys-tem is our commitment to freedom. As you surely all know, the definition of this freedom is generally very hollow and self-centered. It has little to do with the freedom of the children of God.

Many have discovered under communism that less is more. We in the West no longer believe that. We've turned the Gospel into a kind of spiritual capitalism: we want to *get* grace, *we* want to be "saved," we want to *have* security — the private ego wants to go on accumulating more and more. And spiritual possessions are the most dangerous of all.

There is, on the one hand, the truth of community and, on the other hand, the truth of individual freedom. The Church is the only laboratory that can bring these two truths under one roof. Every part of the body of Christ in the whole world has a special gift. You shouldn't doubt yours. But this also means that we have to distinguish quite clearly between what's light and what's darkness, what is genuine freedom and what is false freedom. And this is certainly the responsibility of all of us.

What Makes a Person a Christian?

A Christian is someone who's animated by the spirit of Christ, a person in whom the spirit of Christ can work. That doesn't always mean that we will consciously know what we are doing. As it says in Matthew 25: "When have we seen you hungry? When have we seen you thirsty?" We may have no idea that we do what we do for Christ. But Christ said: "Because you did it, you did it for me." This is the final consequence of the Incarnation of God. The Word is no longer word; it has really become flesh. That means it never depends upon whether we say the right words, but whether we live the right reality. A Christian is someone who's inhabited by the spirit of Christ, which is a gift, as we know, yet a gift that we can say yes to without fully understanding the gift!

The Gradual American Movement
toward Justice

The American Church is not yet converted. Still it's amazing how many people are slowly realizing what's at stake here. I was in a Protestant seminary and a professor there told me that he himself had noticed how denominational differences are becoming less and less important. There are Christian men and women who are moving toward the perspective of justice, and there are others who aren't. That's the most meaningful division. You can be in a college class or in a seminar and discover only after many days, "Oh, you're Catholic. Oh, you're Protestant." The more the focus is on the questions addressed in the Sermon on the Mount, the more irrelevant the historical confessional differences and their formulations are getting. That doesn't mean they were all false, but they have less meaning and concrete significance. The "preferential option for the poor" is now a broadly rediscovered Gospel ideal. It came from the Central and South American Church.

The Perils of the New Communities

There is a danger in spiritual riches. The corruption of the best is the worst of all. Our gift and our sin are two sides of the same coin. Andreas Ebert and I try to present that idea in our book *Discovering the Enneagram*. We can do the right thing for the wrong reasons. But that doesn't mean we shouldn't try to do the right thing. The point is that we always have to be mindful of its dark side too. It's always very humbling when you do that. Everything that becomes an end in itself — except for God — becomes an idol, including Christian community. Maybe that's even one of the reasons why so many communities have fallen apart. We were forced again to press on to a deeper level and to ask: What is faith now?

I compare everything that belongs to the Church with fingers that point to the moon. We're all just means to the end, not the end itself. As soon as we begin to argue about the fingers or to protect the fingers or to quarrel over who has the best fingers, instead of noticing that all these fingers point to the moon, then we're disobeying the First Commandment, which forbids us to create idols. Christian community can become an idol too; even the Bible can become an idol. The pope can be an idol. The sacraments can be idols. And the more spiritual it looks, the more dangerous it is. The spiritual life is a very risky adventure, but what's the alternative?

9

Less Is More —
Paths to a Spirituality
of the Simple Life

❧

F OR THE PAST FOUR YEARS I've been living in the American
Southwest, in New Mexico.[18] It's one of the poorer
states in America, though also one of the most beautiful.
It's a very militarized state (the atomic bomb was invented
there). This state also shares a border with Mexico, so
we have many Latin American refugees staying with us.
I headed out there four years ago to set up the Center
for Action and Contemplation, where we try to educate
people in a spirituality of social justice.

The city of Albuquerque lies in the middle of the desert
and is surrounded by many Indian tribes. That's why it's a
wonderful place for someone on a quest for wisdom. But
it seems wherever one finds positive spiritual energy there
also is negative spiritual energy. The place where the Indians have prayed for centuries is the place where we've
created the instruments of death. And Christians have to
go to precisely this sort of place to reflect on the meaning of the Gospel and to discern light and darkness, good
and evil.

Let's discuss Jesus' teachings about the simple life. Just
this once I would like to tackle this subject in a completely

different way. Of course, we could go through the familiar texts from Luke, Mark, and the Acts of the Apostles, one after the other, where Jesus quite clearly says that we should live simply and poorly in this world. But then it would seem as if the point was simply to convince or inspire people to do what's right. And after twenty years as a preacher I've noticed that sermons and inspirational work in themselves have no long-term effect. We have to find the truth, *really* find it and believe in it *for its own sake.*

All too long we've tried to motivate people through guilt feelings or fear. We've said, "You have to do this or that, otherwise God won't love you." And if we do the thing in question, *we* really don't do it, because there is no free agent there. Head, heart, and gut don't work together, which is the dignified human personhood God seems to be creating. Instead we end up with the immense passivity, resentment, and passive aggressiveness that I find in so many Christian people. We never gave them time to "become a new creation," (Gal. 6:15) but just ordered them or shamed them into compliance. This is not enlightenment or the salvation of any world. It will change nothing because the agent himself or herself has not yet been changed. You can lead people only as far as you yourself have gone, it seems to me.

So let's take a completely different tack. How is it that after two thousand years of meditation on Jesus Christ we've managed so effectively to avoid everything that he taught so unequivocally? This is true of all the churches. *All* of us, for example, have evaded the Sermon on the Mount. *All* of us have evaded the unmistakable teaching of Jesus' teaching on poverty. *All* of us have evaded Jesus' clear directive on nonviolence. *All* of us have evaded his straightforward doctrine of loving your enemies.

Jesus is too much for us. The Church is a kind of collective teenager. Perhaps we're gradually getting ready to let the Gospel talk straight to us. We have always wanted answers, because in an early stage of human life the first thing we need is certainty. But Jesus doesn't offer us any certainties; he offers us a journey of faith. Jesus doesn't give us many answers; he tells us what the right questions are, what questions the human soul has to wrestle with to stumble onto Christ and *the* truth.

Our formulations determine what we're really looking for. Our questions determine what we ultimately find and discover. Answers acquire power too quickly; they often turn our words into ammunition to be used against others. And answers make trust unnecessary, they make listening dispensable, they make relations with others superfluous. Having my answers, I don't need *you* in order to take my journey. I need only my head, my certainties, and my conclusions. It's all private. But Jesus said we have to live in this world so as to be dependent on one another. The real meaning of a poor life is a life of radical dependency, so I can't arrange my life in such a way that I don't need you. We can't do it alone.

We have to avoid several things here: don't trivialize the words of Jesus by asking, for example: "Does he really want that from me?" Let's not reach too hastily for an answer instead of letting ourselves be invited to a process. Don't be quick to generalize by asking, for example, "Where would we be if we all did this or that?" In this way we often create nightmare scenarios and stifle Jesus' real demand on us. For example, when we discuss Jesus' teaching on nonviolence, people say: "Do you mean to tell me that if someone comes into my house with a gun and wants to kill my wife and my children, I shouldn't defend myself?"

At least one reason for this lies in the fact that until now the Gospel has been expounded by a small elite group. I would have to describe this group as mostly made up of educated men, first Europeans and later North Americans. There's no objection to be made per se against these people — I'm one of them myself. But we've had a monopoly for too long. And in this world there is still a whole mass of other people who have other insights. The white man first raises questions of power and control. The questions that we pose to the Gospel are always questions that come out of this bias. That's why we can't hear the question about nonviolence. Christians have needed to justify killing one another. The question about loving one's enemy can't be heard.

But in our time something wonderful is happening. For the first time in its history the Church is becoming truly universal. The Gospel is being reread and rediscovered by altogether different eyes, and in the process altogether different questions are being raised. And because the new readers are approaching the Gospel with completely new formulations of the issues, they are winding up with completely different answers. And even we white men say, "How come we never saw that?"

Let's consider a text from the nineteenth chapter of Luke, the parable of the pounds. I never liked this story. I went to Catholic school, and on the first day of school the priest gave a sermon on it, admonishing us to be good, hard-working pupils. We were expected to get As and Bs but no Cs. We were supposed to be like the first and the second man in the parable, not like the third. That's why the parable always rubbed me the wrong way. I would now like to look at the story and see whether there might not be a completely different approach to it.

The interpretation that I'll present comes from a base community in Central America made up of quite simple and uneducated people who don't consider themselves theological scholars. But this interpretation has come to America and is now being taken over by some of the best theologians. Many of them are convinced that we have finally discovered the true meaning of this text.

And after twenty years as a preacher I've noticed that sermons and inspirational work in themselves have no long-term effect. We have to find the truth, *really* find it and believe in it *for its own sake.*

"He proceeded to tell them a parable, because he was near to Jerusalem, and because they supposed that the kingdom of God was to appear immediately." This is the starting point. These people expect that a simple, unproblematic shift of power is just about to occur. And Jesus tells himself: I need to reach these people. I believe they have no idea what price they'll have to pay. I believe they don't know what God's Kingdom costs.

"He said therefore, 'A nobleman went into a far country to receive a kingdom.'" Like all good preachers, he starts off with a memorable political event, so that every listener knows what he's talking about. Nowadays we think, of course, that when Jesus mentions the word "king," he means God the Father. But in reality this refers to Archelaos, the son of Herod. Jesus' audience knew that Herod's son had gone on a three-year furlough to Rome after becoming king.

Before heading off, Jesus' "nobleman" has ten of his servants summoned and gives each of them ten pounds. "Trade with these till I come." The historical background here is that before he went to Rome, Archelaos appointed viceroys. And he expected these men to collect the same unfair taxes that he had. He wanted them to oppress the poor the same way he had. When he got back, of course, he wanted to rake in the whole profit. Furthermore it's a historical fact that a delegation of the country's inhabitants was sent after him to Rome with the message, "Don't come back; stay where you are." This is exactly what the next verse says: "But his citizens hated him and sent an embassy after him, saying, 'We do not want this man to reign over us.'"

Thus Jesus isn't talking about some sort of rejection of God and God's gifts, but about altogether down-to-earth topics of politics and oppression. The story proceeds: "When he returned, having received the kingdom, he commanded these servants, to whom he had given the money, to be called to him, that he might know what they had gained by trading. The first came before him, saying, 'Lord, your pound has made ten pounds more.'" So this viceroy was just the same sort of cutthroat as Archelaos himself. "And he said to him, 'Well done, good servant. Because you have been faithful in very little, you shall have authority over ten cities.' " What Jesus is saying to his disciples is, "If you play along with their game, they'll reward you for it. The world takes care of its own."

"And the second came, saying, 'Lord, your pound has made five pounds.' And he said to him, 'And you are to be over five cities.' " I used to think that the first two servants were the heroes; but that's a prejudice of the capitalist mind-set. In reality the first two are blackguards, and the third is the hero. "Then another came, saying, 'Lord, here is your pound, which I kept laid away in a napkin; for I was afraid of you, because you are a severe man; you take up what you did not lay down' " — this is precisely the judgment that Jesus passes on the world — " 'and reap what you did not sow.' "

"He said to him, 'I will condemn you out of your own mouth, you wicked servant! You knew that I was a severe man, taking up what I did not lay down and reaping what I did not sow. Why then did you not put my money into the bank, and at my coming I should have collected it with interest?' " The third man is the one who is really prepared to take the consequences of his conviction. Nowadays we would call this "civil disobedience." We would say: He's responding to a deeper truth; and this *deeper* truth always leads us into conflict with the *superficial* truth. "And he said to those who stood by, 'Take the pound from him, and give it to him who has the ten pounds.' "

But now we suddenly hear a hesitant voice from the wings saying, "Lord, he has ten pounds. Why should the rich always get richer, and the poor always get poorer?" The world takes care of its own. But Jesus taught his disciples not to play along with this system. This is the last parable in the Gospel of Luke, which Jesus tells before he enters Jerusalem to be *crucified.* If you want to live the truth, then you must be prepared to pay the price for it. Sometimes it seems that Jesus' only program for social reform is *noncooperation* and *nonidolatry,* which will usually necessitate living a simple life.

In the first three centuries of church history the Gospel spoke primarily (though not exclusively) to those who belonged to the lower classes, not to the middle and upper classes. It was always the little people who trusted it and the people on top who fought it. But in the year 313 Emperor Constantine declared Christianity an established religion in the Roman empire. Overnight we changed, so to speak, from underdogs to top dogs.

In the fifth century St. Hilarion wrote: "Instead, today we fight a more dangerous persecutor, an enemy who flatters us, namely, the mighty Roman emperor. He no longer wounds our backs; he bedecks our chests with medals. He doesn't confiscate our goods; on the contrary, he gives us gifts. He doesn't force us to be really free by locking us up; he sends us into slavery by honoring us in his palace. He doesn't attack us with his resources, but he takes possession of our hearts. He doesn't hack our heads off with the sword, but he kills our spirit with gold. He doesn't officially threaten us with the stake, but he secretly kindles the fire of hell. He doesn't wage any battles against us, but he adores our Christ, so that he can reign unhindered. He confirms Christ so as to deny him in reality. He proclaims unity, but he prevents communion."

We should try to win back our lower place. Jesus says that he has come to preach the Gospel to the poor since in fact they're the only ones who can hear it! They don't have to prove or protect anything. We always have to ask: In what sense are we ourselves rich? What do we have to defend? What principles do we have to prove? What keeps us from being poor and open? The issue isn't primarily material goods, but our spiritual and intellectual goods — my ego, my reputation, my self-image, my need to be right, my need to be successful, my need to have everything under control, my need to be loved. These are the capital sins that Andreas Ebert and I try to describe in *Discovering the Enneagram*.

The words of the Gospel never allow us to live in self-satisfaction. Rather they always make us empty. They always make us repeat the truth of Mary's "Let it be done to me according to *your* word." They allow us to keep our wounds open so we can receive Christ in us. It seems we're quite incapable of welcoming Christ because we're so stuffed full of ourselves. The real thing we have to let go of is our self. We aren't really free until we're free from ourselves.

The subject of a series of cassette tapes that I recorded, "A Spirituality of Subtraction," goes back to the German mystic Meister Eckhart. Meister Eckhart said that the spiritual life has more to do with subtraction than with addition. But in the capitalistic West, we keep climbing higher up the ladder of spiritual success, and we've turned the Gospel into a matter of addition instead of subtraction. What we should do is get ourselves out of the way! Then God will be evident. Then we can easily welcome Christ. We've taken ourselves so seriously, although we're only a tiny moment of consciousness. As a person I'm just a tiny part of creation, a particle that reflects only a fragment of God's glory. And yet that's enough.

It's really that simple. If we have not experienced that connection, knowing that we indeed are a fragment of the Great Flame, we will almost certainly need to accumulate more and more outer things as substitutes for self-worth. This, of course, is the great spiritual illusion. We needn't acquire what we already have.

My second great spiritual teacher, after Jesus, was Francis of Assisi. He spent his whole life trying to become smaller, a "brother of the lower class." He told us that we should always live at the bottom, since only there can we really experience the truth. But this truth is hard to grasp in a world that says, "Life takes place in the center, and not on the periphery."

You need a great deal of faith to believe that there's enough on the margin too, but nevertheless that's been my experience. I have visited many countries in the Third World. There I always found that the poor of this world are often much happier than most of us. They don't need to constantly project their soul onto things, and so they can find it within themselves.

The poor of the world do not have the luxury of assuming that external things will offer them fulfillment. They don't have access to them, so they have to find life at a deeper, immediate, and more simple level. In that, they have a huge head start, and that is probably why Jesus begins his Sermon on the Mount with "How happy are the poor." (Matt. 5:3)

A woman from the Philippines once told me: "Father, we have nothing except God and our community." I believe that's the only thing the Gospel promises us. It offers us a way that leads to God and a way that leads to one another.

But we want security, although the Gospel never promised us security in this world. Jesus also never said that we had a responsibility to make the world secure. Instead he said that we should live in truth. Since the beginning of time every person who comes into the world is born into insecurity. We can't really protect ourselves against this insecurity, which belongs to our humanness, without also ultimately blocking ourselves off from God. Because the truth can reach us only when we find ourselves at a place of dependency, openness, "longing and thirsting."

We men, who seem to be on top, are actually at the very bottom of the trap. At first glance we look like the system's winners, but in reality we're its victims. We're much less free than most women. In America we observe that the women are about fifteen years ahead of us in their development, because they're not so tangled in the lies of the system and not so stuck in the trap of competition and achievement. That's why they have more freedom to trust a deeper wisdom — unless joined in the same male system, which many now are.

It's amazing: Christianity is the only religion that dares to call God a *lamb*. And nevertheless we've spent two thousand years avoiding vulnerability. Paul says straight out, "When I am weak, I am strong." (2 Cor. 12:10) But we're afraid of discovering this sort of strength. We haven't ever been there, and so we doubt it is really strength. And yet it's the only kind of power that the Gospel offers us. The world will never understand this kind of power, but we have to understand it if we really want to be the Church and if the Church wants to have any kind of credibility.

Karl Rahner[19] once said that if by the next century we don't rediscover the mystical roots of Christianity and the connection between the mystical and the political, then we can forget all about Christianity. Because then Christianity is part of the problem rather than part of the solution.

Spirituality and faith have more to do with subtraction, with becoming *less,* than with addition, with becoming *more.* First we have to let go of the *past:* We all carry large packages of guilt around with us. It's clear to all of us what we *didn't* do and what we did *wrong.* But even our guilt feelings can turn into an ego trip. I dragged guilt feelings around with me so long as I had the need to consider myself especially valuable. When I finally let go of the need to feel "worthy," I noticed that my guilt feelings just encircled myself, meaning most of my guilt feelings just served my own ends. I can easily talk myself into guilt feelings over trifles so that I don't have to tackle the really important things.

In the earlier parable, I think Jesus is trying to tell the disciples: There are very big things at stake here, not the hothouse virtues that middle-class Christianity worries over. That kind of Christianity is too privatized, too individualistic, and basically a distraction, because we're constantly engaged in contemplating our navels and never meet Christ. We always encounter only a new version of ourselves and live in a vicious circle of useless guilt feelings.

But the point isn't just to let go of the past; we must let go of the *future* too. We have to let go of fear of the future, our cares and our exaggerated need for security. Finally we also have to let go of the *present,* the need to be something special here and now. If I have too great a need to be loved, then I'm not free and I'm also not saying the full truth, but only a little truth.

> **So let's take a completely different tack. How is it that after two thousand years of meditation on Jesus Christ we've managed so effectively to avoid everything that he taught so unequivocally? This is true of all the churches. *All* of us, for example, have evaded the Sermon on the Mount. *All* of us have evaded the unmistakable teaching of Jesus' teaching on poverty. *All* of us have evaded Jesus' clear directive on nonviolence. *All* of us have evaded his straightforward doctrine of loving your enemies. Jesus is too much for us.**

One of the hardest parts of letting go is giviis straie need to be something. The more positive our self-image, the more dangerous it is. The more pious it is, the more dangerous it is. And the most dangerous thing of all is to be a professional Christian. It was the Pharisees and scribes who killed Jesus, because they had to defend their theology — and in this sort of theology there's no place for the reality of an incarnate Christ. If we're honest, we probably find it a bit disappointing that Jesus Christ came as a completely normal human being.

Letting go of the present means giving up our self-image, our titles, our public image. I think this is one of the many meanings of the First Commandment: "You shall have no other gods before me." What's at stake here are not just false images of God (which mostly serve our purposes), but also comfortable images of ourselves. That's probably what the saints meant when they said we have to move to the place of faith, to the place of self-forgetfulness, of nothingness.

When C. G. Jung was an old man, one of his disciples read John Bunyan's *Pilgrim's Progress*; and he asked Jung, "What has your pilgrimage really been?" And Jung answered: "My journey consisted in climbing down ten thousand ladders so that now at the end of my life I can extend the hand of friendship to this little clod of earth that I am." That's a free man. The word "human" comes from the Latin *humus,* which means earth. Being human means acknowledging that we're made from the earth and will return to the earth. For a few years we dance around on the stage of life and have the chance to reflect a little bit of God's glory. We are earth that has come to consciousness. If we discover this power in ourselves and know that we are God's creatures, that we come from God and return to God, that's enough. You can't grasp this with logic; even this sermon won't convince anyone that this is how it is. You have to experience it yourself, by going on the journey yourself and walking the path yourself. That's why we call our center in New Mexico the Center for Action and Contemplation, because only when we come to the contemplative vision within do we find the real basis of the Gospel.

This is exactly what Jesus does in the forty days in the wilderness: he goes to a place of emptiness. And he fasted for forty days, meaning, he made himself empty. Allow me to paraphrase the dialogue from Matthew's Gospel. Jesus stared down the demon who told him, "You have to be successful." And he answered, "No, I don't need that." When he stood on the pinnacle of the temple, he stared down the second demon, who told him, "You have to be on the right religious track." This demon could quote Scripture! And Jesus said: "Get lost. I don't need this game." Finally he met the demon who told him, "You can do the will of God with the tools of power." But the price of power is surrendering to Satan.[20]

We all have to start from the assumption that our path too leads into the wilderness and that we have to look exactly the same three demons in the eye: the need to be successful, the need to be righteous or religious, and the need to have power and get everything under control. Until we have stared down these three demons within us, there is no possibility of getting out of the wilderness and proclaiming the Kingdom of God. Otherwise we'll always be proclaiming our own kingdom. We use the Gospel to enthrone ourselves, and then the inner and the outer ways split apart. God calls all of us to take the path of the inner truth — and that means taking responsibility for *everything* that's in us: for what pleases us and for what we're ashamed of, for the rich person inside us and for the poor one. Francis of Assisi called this, "loving the leper within us." If we learn to love the poor one within us, we'll discover that we have room for compassion "outside" too, that there's room in us for others, for those who are different from us, for the least among our brothers and sisters.

Less really *is* more. Only those who have nothing to prove and nothing to protect, those who have enough space in them to embrace every part of their own soul, can receive the Christ. And Christ himself will lead us on this path.

Learning to See and to Hear

My primary goal is to preach the great vision of the Reign of God. Then in this context I want to pass along to others an authentic process of hearing. Here the content is not as important as the process itself being launched. It's a new way you can listen to God. The process is designed so that in the end the conclusions you draw will really be your own and not, the conclusions I've grafted onto you. You have to believe the Gospel for yourself. We learn in this process not to take ourselves too seriously, to put ourselves aside, to pull back. And I believe all great spiritual exercises aim at achieving the same thing. Why does Jesus teach us, for example, to love our enemies? So that they'll become Christians? Perhaps — that would be fine, of course — but he probably says it mainly so that *we* may meet those *we* are afraid of, and thus *we* can be liberated from our fear. Many people who have entered missionary service have been converted by the people they went to convert.

And that's why the statement holds that we have to be ready to find Christ where we didn't expect him before. In Matthew 25, the only description of the Last Judgment offered by Jesus, we don't find anybody with a clearly defined theology. But we do find people who have learned to see and hear and pull back. They can grab God with both hands, so to speak. In his discourse on the Last Judgment Jesus says that we'll be judged simply on whether we were able to recognize Christ in the least of our brothers and sisters, not by our observance of the Ten Commandments or by whether we recognized Christ in other members of our denomination. This is the most radical form of conversion I can imagine. I'll repeat: This is a question of seeing. I believe, therefore, that the Gospel imparts to us in the first instance a process and not a specific series of propositions about faith. If we turn the Gospel into a series of dogmas, we'll spend our whole life defending them.

Community Life at the Practical Level

In "New Jerusalem" we did not have a complete community sharing of material goods. We came to the conclusion that that would create more problems than it would solve. But the people in my community had many other creative possibilities of supporting one another, because our life was shared on a very deep level and we trusted one another. Mothers shared child care and gave one another free time. Men shared tools and helped in house repair. They all helped refugees.

In New Mexico we're not an actual "symbiotic" community. This time I'm trying to do things differently. In Cincinnati we built a self-conscious community that calls itself "New Jerusalem." We spent an enormous amount of energy developing the art of community. From that, many people got a vision of the Reign of God and how they could serve the world. But there's still another way to achieve the same thing: to call men and women together who already have a common vision of justice and mission. I'm convinced that community will then appear as a *by-product,* so to speak. But it is not an end in itself.

Today, after four years, I also think this is the better method for our current situation. The topics of concern today are much too big and too problematic: refugees, the homeless, prison reform, nuclear disarmament. When the topics of the Gospel become so real, then we simply know that we need the Body of Christ to discover with one another what's at stake and also how to deal with one another. Perhaps we've watered down the Gospel so much because we only took individuals as our starting point.

Confronting Technology

Centuries ago we forgot how to have a genuine dialogue with technology, and so technology has gone on developing, but not our wisdom. We've divided the world up quite comfortably with religion on the one side and secular things on the other. As a Church we've lost the capacity to hold an authentic dialogue with the secular world, and we've withdrawn to our closed Christian world because we're capable of talking only with people who were already of our opinion anyway. That's why money has the primary say these days, because we've stopped saying anything to money. In other words, it does all the talking, and we do not seem to know how to preserve our human dignity and lead the conversation. It usually leads us. Technology also seems to have the floor in the same way.

This is a vocation that many of you have. Please don't spend the rest of your lives in churches. Use the experience that you've had of the truth and of the Word of God to deidolize the systems of this world. Use this experience to raise critical questions from the standpoint of your faith. Jesus taught us that we should love people and use things. But you and I live in countries that use people and love things. And this reversal has occurred because we didn't manage to reconcile our faith and the world.

Every Friday morning in the neighborhood of our center we hold a prayer vigil in front of the gates of a nuclear laboratory. We don't point the finger threateningly at the people who work there. We hold posters up that raise questions of faith. In the beginning we got a lot of angry gestures and cries of rage. But after three months the situation changed. The workers had learned in the meantime that we weren't their enemies; they sensed we were posing intelligent religious questions out of concern for the world — as brothers and sisters. Last Ash Wednesday they even invited me into the barracks to celebrate Mass there. And some people said, "That guy you're inviting in here is our enemy." But the church was full, and after the service the people stayed an extra hour to talk with me. Now we have a dialogue every month, and I myself can scarcely believe how far we've gotten on this way with one another.

We do not call the people who work there evil. We know that as individuals they're as good as we are and perhaps even better. I still believe that they're participating in something that on the whole and as a system is evil, but as individuals they're good. As Christians we've too long neglected to establish a link between individual and structural sin. We've been busy the whole time denouncing *individual* sin. But it's the *institutionalized* sin that's chiefly responsible for the world's injustice.

Sometimes there are simple people who are wiser than we are. There's another nuclear laboratory in New Mexico, at Los Alamos, where the atomic bomb was invented. Around this region three Catholic Indian tribes are settled. Among the tribes the Catholics are mixed in with those who adhere to their traditional religion. Five years ago, as our bishops were debating whether we should condemn the doctrine of deterrence as morally bad from the Christian point of view, the Indians began quietly to perform an "exorcism" over Los Alamos. With their so-called primitive wisdom they have no doubt that this is the place where the destruction of the world is being prepared. You have to wonder where the real wisdom lies. Our Christ is so great that we know he has no fear of the truth. Hence as Christians we have to have the freedom to integrate psychology, history and theology, anthropology and sociology: we needn't be afraid of anything.

As soon as we've found our center, we no longer have to defend our boundaries. We've spent so many years defending our boundaries because we weren't sure of our center. I personally believe that only contemplative prayer can lead us to our center. So I'll give you a piece of advice that may strike you as peculiar: I encourage you to enter upon a radical inner path of prayer. The place in you that seems to be the most intimate is in reality the most universal and global in scope. At this place you'll find the freedom to confront science and technology and connect them with faith and morality.

Learning from Other Religions

Twenty-five years ago at the Second Vatican Council the bishops composed some wonderful documents. One of the most important of those was on our relationship with non-Christian religions (*Nostra Aetate*). It starts by affirming that "all peoples comprise a single community, and have a single origin.... One also is their final goal, God. His providence, his manifestation of goodness, and his saving designs extend to all people" (no. 1). In the second section, the document quickly affirms that those of other religions are also struggling with the same mystery that Christians are struggling with. It says, "The Catholic Church rejects nothing which is true and holy in these religions. She looks with sincere respect upon these ways of conduct and life, those rules and teachings which, though differing in many particulars from what she holds and sets forth, nevertheless often reflect a ray of that truth which enlightens all people." One wonders what has happened to that courageous wisdom since it was first officially taught in 1965. It is a short but prophetic document worth reading again. History waited thousands of years for such freedom.

I admit that you already have to be very spiritually mature to be at this point. You can't begin here. It might sound strange, but I always emphasize that you have to start conservative. You have to begin somewhere and send down deep roots from that place. We have to go the whole way with Christ, and only then will we meet the cosmic Christ. Then we will no longer need to defend our frontiers so stubbornly, and we can see that truth can be found in the other great world religions too. I know that many people are not ready for this yet, and I have to admit that I myself took a very long time to get to this point. But why else would Jesus say so often: Don't be afraid, don't be afraid! A large percentage of Christians are still afraid, as if God needed us to defend divine truth, as if God needed us to defend God's work. I believe that in reality we don't at all love the Christ who is the Alpha and Omega of history; instead we love a little Jesus whom we can stick in our pocket.

The Meaning of the Spiritual Gifts

As soon as we distance ourselves from the control center of our brains, as soon as we free ourselves from the comfortable principles of our preconceived theology, as soon as we've gotten to the point where we know only that we actually know nothing, then the transcendent can reach us. Then we are no longer caught in the myth of reason, the myth of science. Then we open to the nonrational as well, to grace, to the transcendent, to the burning bush. It's all a matter of seeing.

I believe that God often comes into this world quite unexpectedly, uninvited, and even unwanted. Take the charisms, for example, the many spiritual gifts of healing, tongues, and forgiveness; through them we experience the immediate action of God in this world. They're necessary for us to develop a taste for the holy. It's very sad that in Western Christianity so few people have a genuine sense of the sacred or an authentic access to it, the feeling that

"I'd just like to kneel down." Without this, religion very quickly becomes sterile and rigid.

But on the other hand we can't strive firstly for transcendental or emotional experiences of faith, because if we do they can easily become a cheap substitute for real faith. Faith is ultimately faith, which means to believe and to know — *without* experience and *without* feelings. We might have to spend a whole lifetime walking in darkness, recalling the little we've experienced in the light.

I'll just take the most familiar and widespread charism, "speaking in tongues." It's the least of the spiritual gifts and nevertheless a very important one. Because when we speak in tongues we have to abandon our need for control and our constant need to explain everything. We have to drop the predominance of reason.

There are many indications that praying the rosary became customary in the Catholic Church when speaking in tongues had died out. Moving the fingers with the beads has the same effect: we stop having to understand everything; we simply sit in the presence of the mystery.

Some of the Indians in our region have learned contemplative prayer without calling it that. When they get up in the morning, their mother tells them: "Don't say anything; go to the door that opens to the east. Stand there and look at the rising sun, and just make a slow gesture of welcome." That doesn't sound especially sublime. But I believe it's precisely because of such quiet simple gestures that these people have a sense for the holy. They're ready for God to enter their world. When we lose this openness to the transcendent, then we probably lose contact with the God who is really God.

Letting Go of Emotions

Emotions have an important function in the spiritual life, but we shouldn't become dependent on them. And we should not strive for them for their own sake. We experience a purification through trials, so that we can be freed from our attachment to feelings and not take the transitory emotions too seriously. We have to let go of them, so that really great emotions can come to light, genuine passions that free us for leading a completely different life.

Normally it goes like this: the more we grow in faith, the fewer emotional experiences we'll have. Teresa of Avila, who has written such wonderful things about the dark night of purification, says that she spent eighteen years without one comforting emotion. But afterward she experienced quite deep ecstatic feeling. Many of us are so emotionally overstimulated — we watch so many movies, we hear so much music — that we're no longer capable of the deeper feelings. We're not prepared for the feelings that really convert and change us. That is why some sort of "fasting" experience is so important for us. That's the meaning and the original significance of the forty days of Lent.

Developing a Healthy Sense of Self-Worth

We can't consciously decide to have a positive self-image; I like to say that it happens to us, it "befalls" us. As Christians we can't save ourselves; we get saved. If we go to too much trouble fishing for compliments, then we don't believe the compliments when we get them. The only gifts that heal us are the ones that are voluntarily given. If we play a game in which we have to kiss our girlfriend, then the kiss doesn't feel half as real as the kiss she gives of her own free will. The most important thing we need is a spiritual conversion so that I no longer have to defend my negative *or* my positive image.

What we need here is not excessive self-consciousness but authentic contemplation. When we discover ourselves "hidden with Christ in God," we don't *need* any kind of self-image at all. I hope this doesn't sound too esoteric, because it isn't; it's what happens in true prayer. This is what will happen when we expose ourselves to silence and stop exposing ourselves to the judgments of the world; when we stop continuously "picking up" the energy of others; when we stop thinking about what others think of us and what they take us to be. We are who we are in God — no more and no less.

That's why I have to go into the wilderness, where I let God call me by name to a deeper place. This is the peace that the world can't give. But I promise you that it's also the peace that the world can no longer take from you. This peace doesn't come about because of anything we do right. The point is, we have to discover what we have always been in God. When we get to this place, we will know and love ourselves, in spite of all the negative and opposing evidence. It is the spacious place of the soul. To live there is finally to be at home. This first and final home we carry with us all our lives. God is also at home there, and when we return we will have discovered simplicity.

Notes

1. The material for the original German edition of this book was adapted from lectures and conversations that were translated from English into German and recorded. Those recordings were transcribed and adapted. The translators were Harald Walach, Frank S. Lorenz, and Andreas Ebert. Constanze Keutler-Hagl, Marion Küstenmacher, and Andreas Ebert collaborated on the editorial tasks.

2. Pastor Felix Felix, in *Rundbrief der Diakonischen Gemein-schaft,* Friedensgasse, Basel (March 1990): 12–14.

3. Beat Rüegger, in *Reformiertes Forum* 12 (March 23, 1990): 19.

4. *The Ascent of Mt. Carmel,* I, 13, #10.

5. Material adapted from a talk given in the Church of St. Matthew, Basel, March 7, 1990.

6. Thomas Merton, *The Sign of Jonas* (New York: Harcourt, Brace, 1953), 362.

7. Material adapted from an afternoon colloquium in Basel, March 8, 1990. The audience consisted mostly of members of Christian communities and brotherhoods.

8. Material adapted from a talk given in the Church of St. Matthew, Basel, March 8, 1990.

9. Material adapted from a talk given in the Church of the Cross, Dresden, March 14, 1990.

10. See M. Scott Peck, *The People of the Lie* (New York: Simon & Schuster, 1983).

11. Material adapted from a talk given in the Church of the Cross, Dresden, March 15, 1990.

12. A talk given in Holy Spirit Hall, Nuremberg, March 16, 1990. *Der Nakte Gott* was never translated into English.

13. On the question of why evil has such a strong impulse toward bodies, see M. Scott Peck, *The People of the Lie* (New York: Simon & Schuster, 1983).

14. *When Society Becomes an Addict* (San Francisco: Harper & Row, 1987).

15. Richard Rohr, *Why Be Catholic?* (Cincinnati: St. Anthony Messenger Press, 1990).

16. Material adapted from a sermon given at a service of biblical commentary in the Church of St. Lawrence, Nuremberg, March 18, 1990; published in *Radical Grace: A Newsletter for the Center for Action and Contemplation,* July–August 1989.

17. Material adapted from a talk given in the Old Library, Giessen, March 19, 1990.

18. Material adapted from a talk given in the Peace Church, Darmstadt, March 20, 1990.

19. In 1990, on my forty-seventh birthday, I had the privilege of preaching from the pulpit in Darmstadt. One of my personal heroes, Fr. Karl Rahner, had preached in that pulpit several times. I was reminded of his presence that day and of the big shoes I had to fill.

20. See Matthew 4:1–11; Luke 4:1–13.

About the author

Richard Rohr, O.F.M., is a Franciscan priest of the New Mexico Province. He was the founder of the New Jerusalem Community in Cincinnati, Ohio, in 1971, and, in 1986, the Center for Action and Contemplation in Albuquerque, New Mexico, where he presently serves as Founding Director. The Center is intended to serve a dual purpose, not only as a radical voice for peaceful, nonviolent social change but also as a forum for renewal and encouragement for the individual who seeks direction from and understanding of God's will and love.

Richard was born in 1943 in Kansas. He entered the Franciscans in 1961 and was ordained to the priesthood in 1970. He received his master's degree in theology from Dayton that same year. He now lives in a hermitage behind his Franciscan community in Albuquerque and divides his time between local work and preaching and teaching on all continents. He is well known for his numerous audio and video tapes and for his articles in the Center's newsletter, *Radical Grace*. He is a regular contributing editor/writer for *Sojourners* magazine and recently published a seven-part Lenten series for the *National Catholic Reporter*. He has a best-selling tape series called *The NEW Great Themes of Scripture*. Fr. Rohr has authored several books in the areas of male spirituality, the use of the Enneagram in spiritual direction, and scriptural commentary. He is working on a book on male initiation.

ALSO BY RICHARD ROHR

EVERYTHING BELONGS
The Gift of Contemplative Prayer

Revised & Updated!

Richard Rohr has written this book to help us pray better and see life differently. Using parables, koans, and personal experiences, he leads us beyond the techniques of prayer to a place where we can receive the gift of contemplation: the place where (if only for a moment) we see the world in God clearly, and know that everything belongs.

"Rohr at his finest: insightful cultural critique, with strong connection to the marginalized." — *The Other Side*

THE GOOD NEWS ACCORDING TO LUKE
Spiritual Reflections

Now in paperback!

Grounded in scholarship but accessible to a general audience, this spiritual commentary sheds light on the main themes of Luke's Gospel. Rohr addresses individual concerns, duties, and possibilities, and then connects them to the larger picture of cultural and ecclesial postures, emphases, and values.

"Rohr not only offers a wealth of insight on Luke, but also proclaims a clarion call for us to follow Jesus today."
— *Spiritual Book News*

crossroad

OF RELATED INTEREST

Ronald Rolheiser
THE SHATTERED LANTERN
Rediscovering a Felt Presence of God

The way back to a lively faith "is not a question of finding the right answers, but of living a certain way. The existence of God, like the air we breathe, need not be proven...." Rolheiser shines new light on the contemplative path of Western Christianity and offers a dynamic way forward.

"Whenever I see Ron Rolheiser's name on a book, I know that it will be an amazing combination of true orthodoxy and revolutionary insight — and written in a clear and readable style. He knows the spiritual terrain like few others, and you will be profoundly illuminated by this lantern. Read and be astonished." —Richard Rohr, O.F.M.

Paula D'Arcy
THE GIFT OF THE RED BIRD
A Spiritual Encounter

"To say that *The Gift of the Red Bird* moved me deeply seems inadequate. I wept for its beauty, pain, and joy. It is a powerful testimony to how the Divine woos the soul into a sacred embrace. Paula D'Arcy's vulnerability and courage in narrating her true story of this Divine encounter are remarkable." —Joyce Rupp

crossroad

OF RELATED INTEREST

Henri Nouwen
THE HEART OF HENRI NOUWEN
His Words of Blessing
Edited by Rebecca Laird and Michael J. Cristensen

In commemoration of the 70th anniversary of Nouwen's birth, Crossroad presents this anthology of the best of Henri Nouwen, with selections from *Life of the Beloved, Here and Now, Beyond the Mirror, Finding My Way Home,* and *Sabbatical Journey.*

Henri Nouwen
HERE AND NOW
Living in the Spirit

In these insightful meditations Nouwen shows how God is much closer than we ordinarily realize.

Please support your local bookstore,
or call 1-800-888-4741 for Customer Service.

For a free catalog, write us at

info@CrossroadPublishing.com

crossroad